DEMENTIA AND THE CHURCH:
A PRACTICAL GUIDE

ENDORSEMENTS FOR DEMENTIA AND THE CHURCH

Bishop Dexter Edmund

For so many years there have been a number of subject matters that have been viewed as taboo within our often-insular church communities. It is with great relief and gratitude from my part that this publication brings to the forefront a subject that has affected or will affect all of us in one way or another.

As a pastor, I'm visiting an increasing number of long-time members of our churches who are now in nursing homes dealing with the impact of dementia.

I do not think for one moment that I am fully conversant with the science of this disease, but I do have very personal experiences of my own loved ones and even those who I considered to be mentors and spiritual leaders who I have witnessed firsthand succumb to dementia.

There are those who have, for whatever reason, spiritualised dementia; they believe that spirit-filled believers should not have to deal with this. I take this opportunity to emphatically disagree with this misguided, albeit well-meaning, notion.

The bodies that we now live in were not made to live eternally. As the apostle Paul said, "in this body we groan." For some, the groaning of this body is manifested by dementia. Thank God one day we will have new bodies and will be free from sickness, whether physical or psychological, but until then we will have to confront diseases of all kinds.

I commend Dr Carol Ighofose and her team for having prepared for and executed this much-needed publication, *Dementia and the Church*. It is a scholarly yet very practical handling of the most sensitive of subject matters. It starts with a general overview of dementia, introduces legal information and personal testimonies, and concludes with a glossary of terms, providing the reader with a variety of resources and points of reference.

A very dear uncle of mine was once visited by his own son, and he did not remember who he was. This news saddened me greatly, and yet I believed wholeheartedly that he would remember me if I visited him. After all, this was a man that I loved, a man who I knew loved me and with whom I shared a very special and close bond, a man who would always call me by a special name only shared between the two of us.

When I entered the room with great hope that we would instantly connect, I was horrified that even after much prompting he did not recognize me. My aunt then summarised in one word what dementia is to me and all of us: "It's wicked." Yes, it indeed is—it robs our loved ones of their memories and gives us a front-row seat to witness their suffering.

As more and more members of our churches are impacted by this *wicked* disease, we will be forever indebted to the editorial team that brought the vision of this publication to fruition. I for one will read it often and refer it to others as an invaluable resource.

Bishop Dexter Edmund
Presiding Bishop
Bethel United Church of Jesus Christ (Apostolic), UK and Europe

Bishop Andrew Landell

Wonderful and timely, easy to read and understand, this is a great addition to the Christian toolbox of available resources discussing a subject previously seen as taboo.

The Lord instructed Habakkuk to "write the vision, and make it plain upon tables, that he may run that readeth it" (Habakkuk 2:2).

The fear and panic that arose from the Covid-19 pandemic during Lockdown 1 in 2021 led me to outline my vision to the Bethel Central District Wellbeing team. I requested that Lead Clinician Dr Carol Ighofose, along with her associated medical and educational professionals within the district who educated us on vaccines, put presentations together that would cover the taboo subjects of mental health, specifically of dementia and Alzheimer's disease.

Up until now church members have shied away from speaking up and sharing their experience with dementia based on how they have understood 2 Tim 1:7: "For God hath not given us the spirit of fear; but of power, and of love, and of a sound mind." How could our Lord allow our Christian family members' minds to be attacked by the adversary?

My answer to this doubt is as follows: to remind ourselves that Jesus in Matthew 9:35 "went about all the cities and villages, teaching in their synagogues, and preaching the gospel of the kingdom, and healing every sickness and every disease among the people." He instructed his disciples to do the same in Matthew 10:1—to spread love in our world and embrace those hit by diseases, rather than judge, criticise or avoid them out of misguided fear.

As the old saying goes, "Mighty oak trees from little acorns grow." This presentation on dementia has now been given to a number of churches and church organisations to great acclaim, resulting in the publication of this book to further spread awareness in more church communities and society at large. It is written in plain language to aid readers' understanding, so that medical jargon would no longer be the barrier to knowledge sharing or cause undue fear and anxiety about dementia management. Being informed and educated on the subject helps demystify dementia and debunk the common misconception that the condition is a spiritual attack. It uncovers what it actually is: a disease.

I trust that readers will benefit from this superb collection of practical, professional and personal insight into living with dementia, whether it is from the perspective of the patient or of the carer, by implementing what they have learned into practice.

In the Master's service,

Bishop Andrew Landell
Bishop – Bethel District 5; Bethel United Church of Jesus Christ (Apostolic), UK

Dr Una Davis

I am honoured to have been asked to write a testimonial for *Dementia and the Church: A Practical Guide.*

During the Bethel International Convocation in 2022, Dr Carol and her team gave their presentation on the subject of dementia, which was so brilliantly planned and executed. They were objective, informative and insightful, sufficiently providing the audience with facts, implications, real-life examples and treatment methods.

I had the pleasure of speaking with Dr Carol the other day and was delighted to hear that she was in the process of converting these presentations into a book. The publication of this handy guide on dementia marks a milestone for the collective endeavours and progress made by those working tirelessly in the field of medicine, in the church, and in society at large.

I'm blessed to be a voice of endorsement for this meaningful work and hope that it serves you well as an indispensable resource in your dementia journey.

Best wishes,
Dr Una Davis
Leader, The Treasured Saints Department, Bethel United Church, Apostolic, UK

DEMENTIA AND THE CHURCH:
A PRACTICAL GUIDE

DR CAROL S. IGHOFOSE, DR JOYPHEN HENRY
SANDRA SIMMONDS-GOCAN, DEZRENE JONES-BEEZER
DANIEL SIMMONDS, ELAINE RICHARDS
ELENE MAYNARD-SCANTLEBURY, JACQUELINE NICELY

Copyright Page

Dementia and the Church: A Practical Guide

1st edition published by Dr Carol S. Ighofose, Dr Joyphen Henry et al.

Copyright 2023 © Dr Carol S. Ighofose, Dr Joyphen Henry et al

ISBN: 9798871098790

All rights reserved. Neither this book nor any parts within it may be sold or reproduced in any form without permission.

No part of this book may be reproduced in any form or by any electronic or mechanical means including information storage and retrieval systems, without explicit permission in writing from the authors. The only exception is a reviewer who may quote short excerpts in a review.

The purpose of this book is to educate, inspire and comfort. The views and opinions expressed in this book belong solely to the authors based on their personal experiences and education.

The authors shall be neither liable nor responsible for any loss or damage allegedly arising from any information or suggestion in this book.

DEDICATION

This book is dedicated to all those whose unwavering compassion illuminates the lives of individuals touched by dementia. Your kindness creates signposts and bridges where memory falters, and your love leads a guiding torch through the challenging path. May this book serve as a source of inspiration for your journey and as a testament to your resilience.

"For God is not unrighteous to forget your work and labour of love, which ye have shewed towards his name, in that ye have ministered to the saints, and do minister." -Hebrews 6:10 (KJV)

TABLE OF CONTENTS

Foreword 12
Dementia UK

Introduction: Dementia Has No Boundaries 16
Reverend Dr Joy Henry

Chapter 1: Dementia: An Overview 26
Dr Carol S. Ighofose

Chapter 2: The Regions of the Brain and
How They Are Impacted by Dementia 36
Dr Carol S. Ighofose

Chapter 3: The Role of the Church in Dementia Care 44
Mrs Sandra Simmonds-Gocan

Chapter 4: Caring for the Carer 56
Mrs Dezrene Jones-Beezer

Chapter 5: The Law and Dementia 64
Mr Daniel Simmonds

Chapter 6a: Living with Someone with Dementia 72
Mrs Elene Maynard-Scantlebury

Chapter 6b: Living with Dementia — "Changes" 84
Mrs Jacqueline Nicely

Chapter 7: Risk Factors, Complications,
Prognosis and Management 90
Dr Carol S. Ighofose

Chapter 8: Is There Anything I Can Do to Prevent Dementia? 104
Dr Carol S. Ighofose

Chapter 9: Common Questions and
Answers and Unique Dementia Quotes 120
Mrs Elaine Richards

Chapter 10: Conclusion 132
Dr Carol S. Ighofose

Glossary of Terms 136

Acknowledgments 142
Mrs Elaine Richards

About The Authors 146

FOREWORD

DEMENTIA UK

It is with great pleasure that I present *Dementia and the Church: A Practical Guide* to a global audience. I believe that this guide will be an invaluable resource for churches and other faith communities in the UK and around the world which seek to provide support for individuals living with dementia and their families.

Dementia is a condition that touches the lives of millions, not only those diagnosed with the condition, but also their loved ones, caregivers and communities. In the face of this growing challenge, it is crucial that we find solidarity to promote empathy and adopt practical solutions. In our collective endeavours to raise awareness and initiate positive change, churches play a unique role as places of solace, belonging and spiritual guidance and have the power to make a significant impact in the lives of people affected by dementia.

Dementia and the Church: A Practical Guide is a must-read that delves into the intersection of dementia and faith, recognising the important role that the church can play in supporting individuals on their dementia journey. It offers a wealth of knowledge, practical advice and spiritual insights, empowering faith leaders, volunteers and congregations alike to create dementia-inclusive environments that help dementia patients retain their human dignity and identity through meaningful engagement with their communities.

At Dementia UK, we are dedicated to improving the quality of life for people with dementia and their loved ones through the provision of specialist admiral nursing. We recognise the tremendous importance of addressing the spiritual and emotional needs of those affected by this condition. We commend and admire the authors of this guide for their expertise, compassion and dedication in tackling this often-neglected aspect of dementia care.

Within the pages of this book, readers will find a wealth of guidance on various topics, including ways of understanding dementia from a medical perspective, considering legal aspects of dementia care, enhancing accessibility within places of worship, facilitating effective communication, providing pastoral care, organising dementia-friendly activities, supporting caregivers and benefiting from a healthier lifestyle. On the basis of thorough research, personal experiences and best practice, this guide provides faith communities with useful tools that they need to create a positive environment that fosters understanding, acceptance and support for individuals living with dementia.

I hope that this guide will not only inform and educate but also inspire readers to expand their view and understanding of dementia. By embracing the principles outlined in this book, churches have the opportunity to become a beacon of compassion, resilience and hope for individuals and families affected by dementia.

I would like to extend my heartfelt gratitude to the authors for their excellent contributions and, of course, my deepest appreciation to church leaders, congregations and volunteers for their unwavering commitment to making churches dementia-friendly spaces.

I hope that *Dementia and the Church: A Practical Guide* will serve as a catalyst for change, inspiring churches and other faith communities worldwide to embark on a journey of love for those affected by dementia. Together we can make a difference and create a compassionate and inclusive society for all.

Paul Edwards
Director of Clinical Services
Dementia UK, August 2023

INTRODUCTION:

DEMENTIA HAS NO BOUNDARIES

REVEREND DR JOY HENRY

Dementia is one of the most feared diseases and the most pressing concerns in global society. Its prevalence makes it highly likely that you are directly acquainted with someone living with dementia or have at least heard of a person affected by it. The condition affects not only the persons diagnosed and their immediate circles of families and carers, but also governments, scientists, medical practitioners and health organisations across the globe on a much larger scale.

Dementia is the seventh leading cause of death worldwide and a major cause of disability.[1] Even though there is presently no proven pharmaceutical cure for dementia, the UK government is determined to make England a world leader in fighting dementia and has pledged to invest in research to tackle the problem by finding an effective cure. The UK is on the verge of a new dawn for their battle against dementia; as we speak, drugs are being developed to slow the progress of cognitive decline in early-stage Alzheimer's patients.[2] If successful this breakthrough could largely facilitate a more positive outlook on the future for dementia patients, but the real hope also lies in putting trust in God who created all people in His image and has the power to heal.

God has created human beings to be relational—to live alongside and love one another. Every person living with dementia wants to be remembered and be loved for who they are as an individual regardless of their condition, rather than cruelly and one-dimensionally labelled as the person with dementia. Different societies and cultures naturally have different concepts of the disease, which has impacted on how people with dementia are treated across the world. As God's agency, the church should be cautious and avoid being influenced by false perceptions of dementia prevalent in our world that stigmatise and often exclude patients from mainstream society. Dementia comes in not one but multiple forms that are medically recognized as distinct types that manifest under different circumstances, which will be explained in further detail in later chapters.

Dementia is not simply a direct result of old age even though longevity may be a contributing factor; it is a neurological condition that affects the brain cells, which leads to cognitive impairment including memory loss, uninhibited behaviour and loss of capacity to make decisions. It is predicted that there will be over 1 million people living with dementia in the UK by 2025 and this figure is likely to rise to 1.6 million by 2040 and 2 million by 2051.[1,3,4] People from certain ethnic minority groups are also at a greater risk of dementia than their white counterparts; for instance, African Caribbeans, Africans and South Asians living in the UK have a higher vulnerability of living with dementia. The number of ethnic minorities with dementia in England and Wales was 25,000 in 2013 and is predicted to rise to approximately 50,000 by 2026.[5] Ethnic minorities access medical help much later than other groups.[6] This book will highlight some of the key risk factors that contribute to the increased prevalence of dementia and the perceived reluctance to seek help among these groups. In addition, studies have indicated that women are at a higher risk of dementia than men; 65% of people living with dementia in the UK are women and dementia is the leading cause of death for women.[4,7]

It is, however, important to note that dementia does not discriminate; despite the higher probability in certain groups as discussed above, it affects men and women, Christians and non-Christians, black and white, rich and poor alike. One out of every three people born in 2015 will live with dementia.[8] The reality is that no one knows or has the ability to predict *who* will live with dementia—that is the uncertainty that we face today. This book, therefore, is designed to help ease the anxiety towards the unknown by raising awareness of dementia and providing a practical list of important, time-sensitive actions to be taken before dementia sets in, including putting in place a power of attorney and making a will. Furthermore, this book provides tips on how to improve health, such as through healthy eating, early access to medical healthcare, exercise (physical and mental) and prayer. The authors are proponents of dementia whose aim is to equip readers with knowledge and a better understanding of what it means to suffer from dementia.

Despite the importance of having steadfast belief in the power of prayer and faith, it is crucial that medical help be sought early, not only for the well-being of the patients, but also for the sake of their families and caregivers. Early assessment allows access to medical treatment and support, and early access to medical care in turn allows the patient to have a treatment plan that reduces the risk of likely complications associated with the disease and hence an overall better quality of life. It helps the individual become aware of the symptoms and of what to expect as gradual deterioration in intellectual capacity takes place. Individuals with dementia can access information on dementia earlier and gain a better understanding of the condition, which can help dissipate their own fears as well as cultural biases and allows them to plan for the future and to develop a positive response to the otherwise anxiety-inducing prospect of living with dementia. Dementia is not just an issue for the individual and their families but one for the church, which should seek to hold dialogue with medical experts and dementia friendly organisations to better understand the disease and to find positive ways to support individuals and families dealing with dementia. A late diagnosis could mean a lesser quality of life for the individual and loss of opportunities to assess medical intervention that might have delayed progression of the disease. It could also be a challenge for caregivers who have not had the opportunity to prepare for the role of a caregiver and are left to simply juggle different roles on their own.

In many cases, caregivers of individuals with dementia also require medical help. Christian caregivers may have a coping strategy based on the application of prayer and Scripture, yet they too are still at risk of poor health because of their high-stress lifestyle. Hypertension, diabetes and fatigue are some of the physical problems they are likely to experience. It poses even more issues along the gender line as women caregivers are less likely to receive support than male caregivers even though women are known to provide 70% of care hours for people with dementia, which supports the claim that dementia has a "disproportionate impact on women."[1] This gender inequality must be addressed to ensure that women caregivers have a higher quality of life as they care for loved ones.

Apart from the timely access to medical care, dementia patients should also be able to reach out to and receive support from their church communities. Such support could be in the form of enabling people with dementia to participate in church activities until they are no longer able to continue. However, do keep in mind that we must monitor the individual's cognitive capacity and ability to participate at all times. Regular communication with the family and caregivers will help to determine the progression of dementia and the appropriateness of their engagement. Dementia diagnosis does not imply that the patient cannot participate in church services, but care should be taken when considering their involvement. As dementia progresses, memory is likely to fail, which increasingly impairs their abilities to actively partake in the services or any other activities. It is imperative that churches be dementia-friendly places where people living with dementia can feel loved with a sense of belonging rather than rejected or excluded. A church community, as caregivers, should advocate for and promote justice and inclusion and oppose all forms of negativity that marginalise people with dementia, irrespective of gender and ethnicity. The church has an important role in the lives of people with dementia who should never be denied their human dignity. The church, in representing Christ, becomes the hub where people with dementia are welcomed and treated with love, kindness and compassion; in doing so the church mirrors Jesus' ministry, reaching out to the sick and the marginalised. The work of the church must extend beyond the walls of the church building and into society on a larger scale since some dementia patients who used to be part of church communities may no longer attend church services and events in a more advanced stage of the disease. The church should be intentional in its Christian ministry for people with dementia and develop good practices that will reveal God's unwavering, unconditional love for them. Visits often take place in individuals' homes or care homes; although they might be challenging due to reasons including embarrassment, they are necessary because to care for someone living with dementia is to enact the Good News of Jesus in practical terms. The golden rule is service, "doing to others whatever you would like them to do to you" (Matthew 7:12).

There are many misconceptions about dementia, which I hope this book helps to dismantle. The authors have provided useful information to reiterate that dementia is a condition that can affect anyone at any given time. It is neither a result of unconfessed sins or demonic possession nor divine punishment. Dementia is like any other disease, such as diabetes, asthma and hearing impairment and therefore should not be seen as a taboo. Dementia does not mean hopelessness; Christians must continue to hold on to their unwavering trust in God as their ultimate healer and to believe that He can heal, if not in this physical world, then undoubtedly in heaven. The people of God can take hope, for they shall eventually rest from their sufferings. When our Lord shall appear, believers in Christ shall be like him (1 John 3:2). The believer's hope is in Christ in this life and the afterlife (1 Corinthians 15:19).

Should we worry when our loved ones lose the capacity to remember to pray or to do the right thing? What if they become aggressive or behave in ways unacceptable for a sanctified believer—what should we do then?

We should pray and spend time with them reading Scripture and singing their favourite hymns. Their history is important; therefore, we must help them remember their past by going through their memory boxes containing keepsakes (e.g., holiday photos or family albums) or serving them their favourite meal.

Holy Communion should not be withheld from individuals living with dementia despite their loss of memory and inability to process the reason for the sacrament. Holy Communion is not dependent on the individual's ability to remember, but rather on the community of believers coming together to be in communion with God and with one another. Persons living with dementia may surprise you with certain behaviours, but do not judge them or hide them away. The damaged and dying brain cells are the root cause for their behaviour, which means you cannot hold them responsible for their actions over which they lack control.

They remain God's children. Dementia cannot take away their birthright in Christ. He died for them the same way he did for those unaffected by the condition; he sanctified and baptised them with the Holy Ghost. Believers living with dementia remain the same people they were before the symptoms began manifesting. Dementia makes no difference to the fact that they are loved by God all the same. They are His precious treasure, and one day He will free them from dementia and take them with Him to live forever in the mansion He has prepared for them (John 14:1-3).

God's people are always in God's memory. He will never forget them.

REFERENCES

1. World Health Organization. Dementia. World Health Organization. Published March 15, 2023. Accessed July 2023. https://www.who.int/news-room/fact-sheets/detail/dementia
2. Devlin H, correspondent HDS. UK on verge of new dawn for dementia treatments, says taskforce chair. *The Guardian*. https://www.theguardian.com/society/2023/apr/26/uk-on-verge-of-new-dawn-for-dementia-treatments-says-taskforce-chair. Published April 26, 2023. Accessed July 2023.
3. Dementia guide. National Health Service. Published December 21, 2017. Accessed July 2023. https://www.nhs.uk/conditions/dementia/?tabname=symptoms-and-diagnosis
4. Alzheimer's Research UK. The Impact of Dementia on Women. Alzheimer's Research UK. Published May 2022. Accessed July 2023. https://www.alzheimersresearchuk.org/wp-content/uploads/2022/05/The-Impact-of-Dementia-on-Women-ARUK-report.pdf
5. All-Party Parliamentary Group on Dementia. *Dementia Does Not Discriminate: The Experiences of Black, Asian and Minority Ethnic Communities*.; 2013. Accessed July 2023. https://www.alzheimers.org.uk/sites/default/files/migrate/downloads/appg_2013_bame_report.pdf
6. Mukadam N, Cooper C, Livingston G. Improving access to dementia services for people from minority ethnic groups. *Current Opinion in Psychiatry*. 2013;26(4):409-414. doi:https://doi.org/10.1097/yco.0b013e32835ee668
7. Prince M, Ali GC, Guerchet M, Prina AM, Albanese E, Wu YT. Recent global trends in the prevalence and incidence of

dementia, and survival with dementia. *Alzheimer's Research & Therapy.* 2016;8(1). doi:https://doi.org/10.1186/s13195-016-0188-8

8. Lewis F. Estimation of Future Cases of Dementia from Those Born in 2015. Office of Health Economics. Published October 5, 2015. Accessed July 2023. https://www.ohe.org/publications/estimation-future-cases-dementia-those-born-2015

CHAPTER 1:

DEMENTIA: AN OVERVIEW

DR CAROL S. IGHOFOSE

Once upon a time, there were two devout Christians named Albert and Sheila. As members of the Bethel United Apostolic Church in England, UK, and as husband and wife, they walked together in faith for many years, finding solace and strength in their relationship with God and His Word.

As they entered their golden years, they encountered a daunting challenge: dementia.

Albert, a loving husband and father, was diagnosed with Alzheimer's disease, the most common type of dementia. He began to forget simple things like where he put his keys or what day of the week it was. Sheila, his faithful wife, noticed the changes and turned to faith for guidance. She clung to the words of Philippians 4:6-7, which reminded her to "not be anxious about anything, but in everything, by prayer and petition, with thanksgiving, present [her] requests to God." She poured out her heart to God, seeking His strength and wisdom to navigate this difficult journey.

Some church members were understanding and compassionate and offered their support and prayers. They visited Albert and Sheila, engaged in heartfelt conversations, and reminded them of God's enduring love, adhering to James 1:27, which called on believers to "look after orphans and widows in their distress." While their help played a vital role in the couple's experience of grappling with dementia, many others in their church community failed to respond with the same empathy; they struggled to understand the complexities of dementia and distanced themselves from Albert and Sheila. Some of them even quoted 2 Timothy 1:7—"For God hath not given us the spirit of fear; but of power, and of love, and of a sound mind"—as a means of substantiating their claim that Christians should not suffer from dementia.

This ostracisation as a result of the lack of awareness left them feeling isolated and forgotten; they hoped that the church would soon remember Galatians 6:2, which instructs believers to "carry each other's burdens," and live by those words.

But Albert and Sheila held fast to their faith amidst these challenges, clinging to the promises of God. They sought reassurance in Isaiah 40:31: "But those who hope in the Lord will renew their strength. They will soar on wings like eagles; they will run and not grow weary." Moreover, Sheila studied 2 Timothy 1:7 and was blessed with revelation from God regarding the true meaning of this scripture that she realised was spoken in the context of Paul's encouragement to a young and timid Timothy. The essence of the scripture is that God makes us spiritually powerful and equips us to use authority boldly (1 Corinthians 2:4); to always demonstrate love and kindness (Galatians 5:22); and to practise self-discipline or sound mind, which is referred to as having a 'wise head' (Galatians 5:23).

To navigate their daily lives, Albert and Sheila relied on their faith to come up with practical solutions. For example, they created memory aids infused with biblical verses, sticking them on the walls of their home. Each time Albert would forget, Sheila gently reminded him of God's promises, fostering a sense of peace and security. They embraced the wisdom of Proverbs 3:5-6: "Trust in the Lord with all your heart and lean not on your own understanding; in all your ways submit to him, and he will make your paths straight."

Their journey with dementia was undeniably challenging, but their faith served as an anchor in the storm. Even when Albert could no longer remember Sheila's name, he would often sing hymns that he had known by heart for years. These melodies resonated deep within his soul, reminding him of God's presence and filling their home with serenity.

As they walked through the challenges and revelations that dementia had brought upon their shared life, Albert and Sheila discovered that their faith had the power to transform their perspective. It granted them the ability to find joy in the simplest moments and to cherish each day as a precious gift from God. They clung to Romans 8:18, which proclaims that "our present sufferings are not worth comparing with the glory that will be revealed in us."

In the end, the church's role in their experience both served as a source of strength and posed a great challenge. The positive examples of compassion and support offered a lifeline, empowering Albert and Sheila to believe that they were not alone. Yet the negative experience of isolation also reminded them of the importance of true Christian fellowship.

Albert and Sheila held on to their faith, allowing it to shape their response to dementia. Their story serves as a testament to the transformative power of faith, even in the face of life's most daunting trials. They inspired others to grow closer to God, and as she became aware of new breakthroughs in the ongoing research on dementia, particularly Alzheimer's disease, Sheila also encouraged and empowered the younger members of their family to endeavour to take the best care of their entire being—spirit, soul and body.

The preceding account is a fictitious but realistic one. In this book, we will find out the ways in which the account resembles or differs from individual experiences with dementia in reality.

This overview serves to provide an outline that closely mirrors the National Institute for Health and Care Excellence (NICE) Guideline on Dementia. It covers all the important areas concerning dementia that should be considered as individuals like Albert and Sheila begin their journeys.

WHAT IS DEMENTIA?

Dementia is a condition where a person experiences **progressive** and **irreversible** symptoms that affect their thinking, behaviour and ability to function day to day. It is an umbrella term used for a group of brain disorders, similar to the use of the word 'fruit' to describe mangoes, apples, pears, grapes, etc. It is worth noting that dementia is categorised as a neurocognitive disorder, not a mental illness. The different types of disorders under the overarching category of dementia are briefly discussed later in this chapter.

The symptoms of dementia fall into three categories:

- **Cognitive impairment**: difficulty retaining memory, language, attention, orientation, logic and problem-solving skills
- **Psychiatric or behavioural disturbances**: changes in personality and lack of control over emotions and social behaviour; depression, agitation, hallucinations and delusions
- **Disruptions in daily activities**: trouble carrying out basic tasks, such as driving, shopping, eating and dressing

To receive a diagnosis of dementia, a person must show **impairment in at least two cognitive areas**, such as memory, language, spatial skills, or executive function. This impairment should lead to a **noticeable and progressive decline** from a previously higher level of functioning that is manifested in their usual activities or work, and cannot be explained by other major mental health conditions. Consciousness should not be clouded as in the case of acute confusional state or delirium. Memory loss is typically experienced for recent events; long-term memory can be remarkably intact. It is important to note that this decline is not simply a result of normal ageing.

When dementia occurs before the age of 65, it is referred to as **early-onset or young-onset dementia** and **late-onset dementia** after age 65.

Mild cognitive impairment (MCI) is a condition where a person experiences cognitive difficulties that do not meet the criteria for a dementia diagnosis. In MCI, only one cognitive area may be affected, or the impact on daily activities may be minimal.

HOW COMMON IS DEMENTIA?

Dementia is a condition that affects millions of people worldwide. Approximately 55 million individuals have dementia, with 10 million new cases each year.[1] In the United Kingdom alone, it is estimated that nearly 885,000 older adults aged 65 years and over were living with dementia as of 2019. With ageing being the main risk factor for dementia, this number is expected to rise to almost 1.6 million by 2040 because life expectancy is increasing over time. Between 2019 and 2040, the number of individuals aged 65-74 years in the UK is projected to increase by 20% while the number of people aged 85 years and over is expected to rise by 114%. When looking specifically at the prevalence of dementia among older individuals in the UK, it is estimated to be 7.1%, which means approximately 7 out of every 100 older people are living with dementia.[2]

Late-onset dementia in older age groups has varying prevalence rates across different age categories after the age of 65. As individuals age, the prevalence appears to increase. To provide a practical numerical explanation:

- For individuals aged 60-64 years, approximately 1 out of every 100 (or 1%) is affected.
- For those aged 70-74 years, it rises to approximately 3 out of every 100 (or 3%).
- Among those aged 80-84 years, it further rises to approximately 11 out of every 100 (or 11%).
- By the time individuals reach the age of 95 years and over, an astonishing 41 out of every 100 (or 41%) are affected by late-onset dementia.[2]

In terms of the severity of dementia, it is estimated that there are 127,000 individuals with mild dementia, 246,000 with moderate dementia and 511,000 with severe dementia in the UK. Surprisingly, around 1 in 20 people with dementia are under the age of 65, showing that it can affect individuals at various stages of life.

Unfortunately, a significant proportion of people with dementia remain undiagnosed. Estimates suggest that between 29% and 76% of individuals with dementia or suspected dementia in primary care settings have not received a formal diagnosis.

These statistics shed light on the prevalence of dementia, both globally and within the UK, placing an emphasis on the urgent need for increased awareness, support and resources to address this growing health challenge.

WHAT ARE THE CAUSES AND TYPES OF DEMENTIA?

Dementia may be considered 'Brain Failure'. It is mainly caused by diseases that slowly damage and disrupt the nerve cells in the brain, the neurotransmitters (chemicals that allow messages to be transmitted across brain cells) and sometimes the spinal cord. The most common types of dementia are:

Alzheimer's disease (AD) (up to 50-75% of cases): This is the most common type of dementia, characterised by the shrinking of the brain cortex and the accumulation of abnormal protein plaques and tangles in the brain. These abnormal proteins are referred to as 'tau' and 'amyloid' and lead to the progressive destruction of neurons (brain cells). Due to the damaged neurons, there is also a decrease in neurotransmitters. AD can occur alongside other forms of dementia and may have a genetic cause.

Vascular dementia (VD) (up to 20% of cases): This type of dementia happens when the brain doesn't get enough blood supply. It can be caused by different problems in blood vessels, such as blockages or bleeding resulting from strokes. Symptoms may include temporary neurological problems, difficulty walking and loss of control over urination. People with vascular dementia can experience depression, delusions and emotional shifts as it progresses. Vascular dementia can sometimes be genetic, especially when it occurs at a younger age.

Dementia with Lewy bodies (DLB) (10-15% of cases): DLB is a common type of dementia in older adults and has similarities to Alzheimer's disease. It is characterised by changes in thinking that can fluctuate, seeing things that aren't there (visual hallucinations), and movement problems similar to Parkinson's disease. Abnormal protein deposits called Lewy bodies are found in the brain. DLB is often considered part of a broader group of diseases known as Lewy body diseases, which also include Parkinson's disease dementia.

Frontotemporal dementia (FTD) (2% of cases): FTD is a significant type of dementia, especially in younger individuals. It affects the front and/or side parts of the brain. Some forms of

FTD can run in families, and it usually begins around the age of 60. However, it can occur earlier or later.

Mixed dementia refers to an individual's experience of a combination of two or more types of dementia simultaneously. It occurs when different causes or types of dementia coexist, often leading to a more complex and challenging clinical picture. The most common form of mixed dementia is a combination of Alzheimer's disease and vascular dementia.

There are **other conditions that can also cause dementia**, such as Parkinson's disease, progressive supranuclear palsy, Huntington's disease, prion diseases like Creutzfeldt-Jakob disease (also known as mad cow disease), normal pressure hydrocephalus, chronic subdural hematoma, benign tumours, metabolic and hormonal disorders, vitamin deficiencies (like B12 and thiamine), infections (such as HIV and syphilis), inflammatory and autoimmune disorders and temporary memory problems caused by epilepsy.

These different types of dementia show us that many different conditions can affect the brain and cause problems with memory and thinking. In the next section, we will take a fun route of examining and learning the major parts of the brain.

CHAPTER 2:

THE REGIONS OF THE BRAIN AND HOW THEY ARE IMPACTED BY DEMENTIA

DR CAROL S. IGHOFOSE

HOW TO LEARN THE MAJOR PARTS OF THE BRAIN QUICKLY - USING YOUR HANDS

Learning the names and functions of the major parts of the brain may seem daunting at first, but it is easier than you'd think! Adapted from Susan J. Shapiro's "The Ultimate Portable Brain Model", this method helps you easily visualise and remember each part of the brain by using your hands as a guide.[3] Understanding how dementia can impact these regions allows us to better comprehend its effects on one's cognition, emotions, bodily functions, and daily activities.

Try the following steps:

1. *Stretch out your hands in front of you. Notice how the skin on the dorsum (back) of your hands is darker than on the palms.*
2. *Now, make a fist with each hand, with your thumbs stretched out over the nails of your other fingers. Then cross your wrists and join the backs of your hands so they touch. Note how the parts of your fists facing you look like two eyes!*

Now let us walk you through what each of these shapes represents:

The Cortex: In the first step of the exercise, the skin on the dorsum of your hands represents the outer layer of the brain, known as the cortex or grey matter. It is slightly darker because it contains the neuronal cell bodies called soma. These parts of the brain cells contain the cells' nuclei and keep the neurons (cells) healthy and functioning. In dementia, the cortex may shrink, leading to cognitive decline.

The White Matter: The white bones covered by muscles inside your hands represent the white matter of the brain. White matter is made up of neuron (cell) axons, which carry information from one neuron to another. It helps in communication and information processing.

CORTEX / GREY MATTER

- Outside part of the brain
- Darker because it is lined with neuronal cell bodies (AKA SOMA), which keep the neurons healthy and functioning.

WHITE MATTER

- made up of neuron (cell) axons
- carry information between neurons (they never really touch-just like your bones!)
- help in communication and information processing.

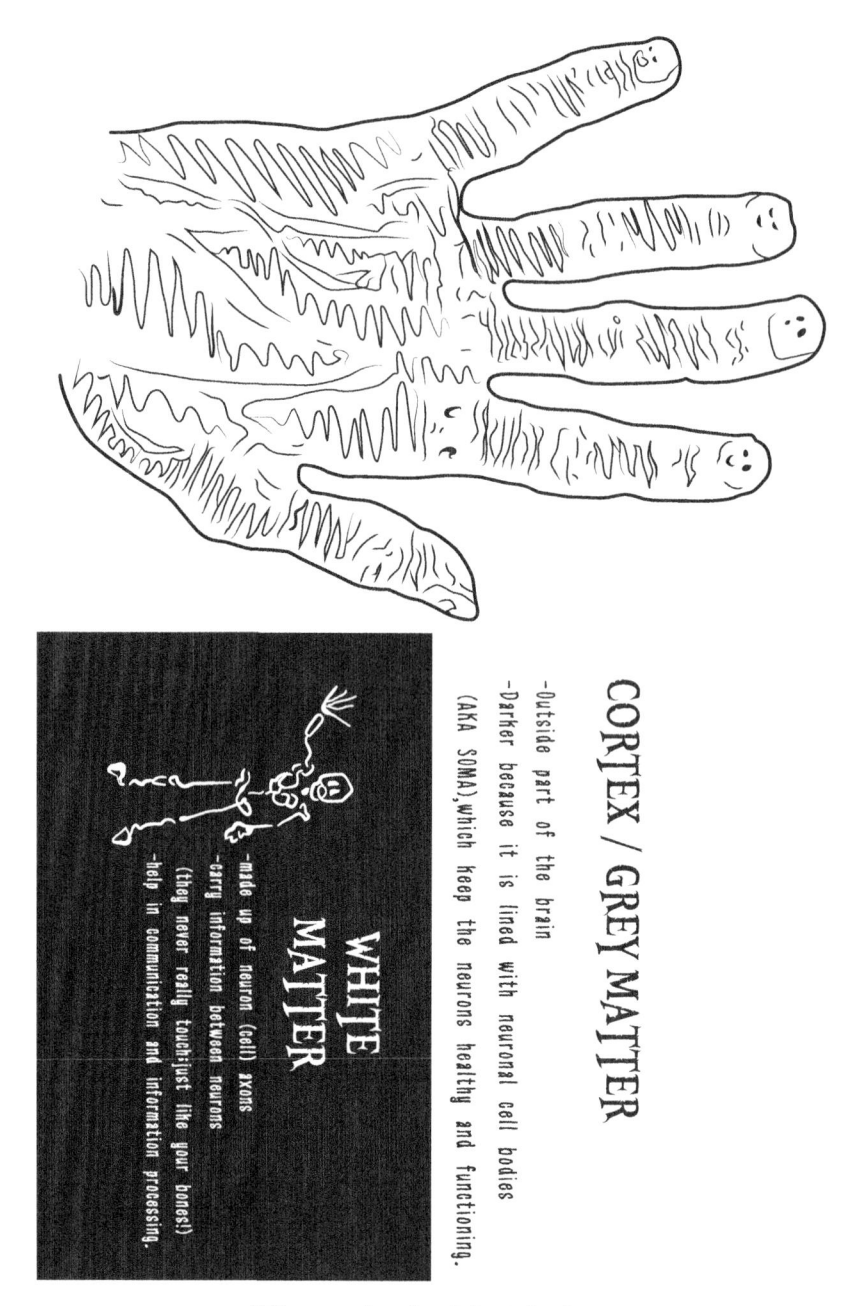

*Illustration by Isio Ighofose

Dementia and the Church: A Practical Guide | 39

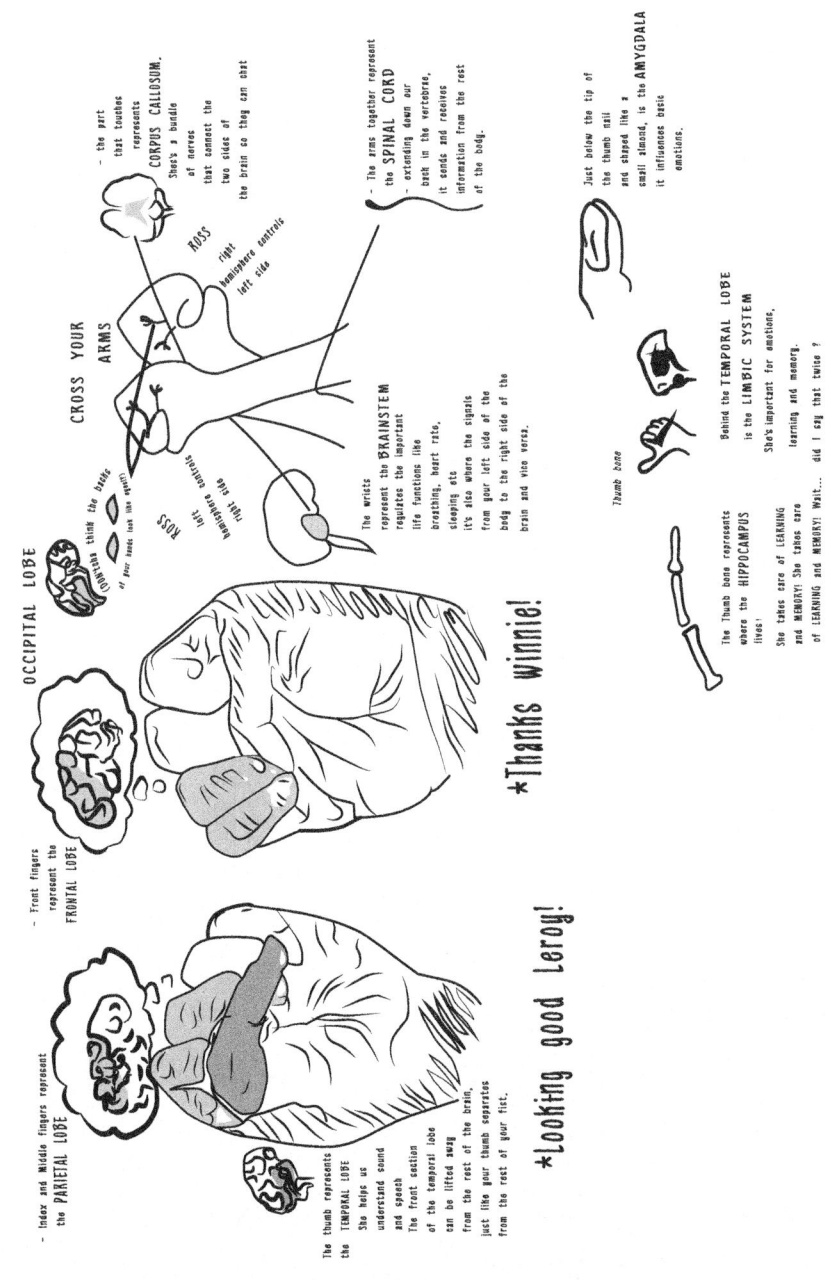

*Illustration by Isio Ighofose

The Corpus Callosum: In the second step of the exercise, the area of contact between the backs of your hands represents the corpus callosum. It is a bundle of nerves that connects the two hemispheres of the brain, allowing them to communicate with each other. In dementia, the corpus callosum may be affected, disrupting interhemispheric communication.

The Brainstem: Your crossed wrists symbolise the brainstem, which sits at the bottom of the brain. It regulates essential functions like breathing, heart rate, sleeping, and eating. The brainstem also plays a role in the crossover of signals between the right and left sides of the brain. Dementia can impact the brainstem, leading to disruptions in vital bodily functions.

The **Spinal Cord**, represented by your arms together, extends down your back and sends and receives information from the rest of your body.

The Frontal Lobe: Imagine your folded front fingers—your little and ring fingers—representing the frontal lobe. This part of the brain, located behind your forehead, is responsible for complex abilities such as planning, decision-making, and emotional control. In dementia, the frontal lobe may deteriorate, affecting executive functions and emotional regulation.

The Parietal Lobe: Extend your index and middle fingers while holding your fists, and you'll visualise the parietal lobe. It integrates sensory information from your body, contributing to your sense of space, navigation, and touch. Dementia can impact the parietal lobe, affecting sensory processing and spatial awareness.

The Occipital Lobe: Look at the sides (I think 'back' or 'part' of your fists facing you that resemble a pair of eyes. These eyes represent the occipital lobe, located in the back of the brain, is responsible for visual information processing. Dementia may cause damage to the occipital lobe, which can lead to visual impairments and difficulties in interpreting what we see.

The Temporal Lobe: Your thumb can represent the temporal lobe, which is responsible for speech and sound comprehension. The front section of the temporal lobe can be lifted away from the rest of the brain, just like your thumb separates from the rest of your fist. Dementia can affect the temporal lobe, leading to difficulties in understanding speech and sounds.

The Limbic System: Inside the temporal lobe lies the limbic system that is responsible for emotions, learning and memory. In dementia, the limbic system may be affected, resulting in emotional and memory disturbances. The amygdala and the hippocampus in the limbic system are key areas that relate heavily to dementia, as explained below:

The amygdala, represented by the part just below the tip of the thumb nail and shaped like a small almond, influences basic emotions.

The hippocampus, best represented by the bone of your thumb, plays a crucial role in learning and memory. In Alzheimer's disease, this region is among the first to be affected, leading to difficulties in forming new memories and eventually in recalling past events. Some studies have shown that engaging in some beneficial activities like puzzles, reading and learning new skills can help stimulate the hippocampus.

Individuals with dementia, particularly Alzheimer's disease, commonly retain the ability to recall past memories while struggling to recall recent memories, as was Albert's experience in our opening anecdote. This phenomenon can be attributed to the selective impairment of brain regions associated with memory formation and retrieval.

As stated above, the hippocampus is a key structure in the brain responsible for encoding new memories and also one of the first areas to be affected by Alzheimer's disease. As a result, the formation of new memories becomes increasingly difficult. However, other brain regions involved in long-term memory, such as the temporal lobe and the association cortex, remain relatively intact in the early stages of the disease. This preservation allows individuals to access and retrieve memories stored in these regions, including nostalgic songs, hymns and familiar experiences from their past. These memories often evoke positive emotions and provide a sense of comfort and familiarity, offering an escape from the challenges of the present.

Family and friends can use music, photographs or activities related to the past to engage and connect with their loved ones, sharing moments of joy amidst the difficulties of dementia. We saw Sheila benefitting from this phenomenon in her endeavours to cope with the challenges that her husband's dementia presented.

Knowing the roles and functions of each brain region allows us to understand the physical and mental impairment experienced by dementia patients. It serves as a reminder of the intricate web that forms our identity and highlights the profound impact dementia has on this delicate tapestry.

REFERENCES FOR CHAPTERS 1 & 2

1. Dementia. NICE CKS. Published 2022. Accessed 2023. https://cks.nice.org.uk/topics/dementia
2. Dementia. World Health Organization. Published March 15, 2023. Accessed July 2023. https://www.who.int/news-room/fact-sheets/detail/dementia
3. Harding M. Dementia. Patient. Published May 22, 2014. Accessed July 2023. https://patient.info/doctor/dementia-pro
4. Mattu A. How to learn major parts of the brain quickly. Youtube. Published January 17, 2017. Accessed July 2023. https://youtu.be/FczvTGluHKM

CHAPTER 3:

THE ROLE OF THE CHURCH IN DEMENTIA CARE

MRS SANDRA SIMMONDS-GOCAN

Dementia is an umbrella term that collectively refers to diseases that affect one's memory, which usually happens in older age groups and can become worse over time.[1]

There are many older saints in our church, whom our Presiding Bishop Edmund respectfully likes to call the Treasured Saints and always reminds us to treat with extra care. It is therefore important to have a written guideline on how to look after our elderly folks, especially the ones with dementia.

As I grew up in the church, I observed that a lot of the elderly saints became more agitated and short-tempered. It used to confuse me when they asked what I was doing there as if they had suddenly forgotten about me. I have since learnt that we can actively help our elderly saints who are experiencing memory loss induced by dementia; I will outline various ways to support our brethren in this chapter.

Our Treasured Saints with dementia can experience the following symptoms, according to NICE Guidelines[2]:

- Difficulty remembering recent events
- Poor concentration
- Difficulty recognizing people/objects
- Poor organisational skills
- Confusion
- Disorientation
- Problems with decision making

If any of these symptoms applies to you, the Alzheimer's Society recommends that you speak to your GP as soon as possible to get a diagnosis. Besides dementia, other illnesses—such as infections, thyroid problems, circulatory issues, vitamin deficiency, menopause, sleep apnea, stress and depression—can be the cause of memory loss. If you contact the GP as soon as possible for support, the cause can be identified and addressed without delay. If you are diagnosed before the symptoms of dementia fully take effect, tell someone you can trust, such as friends/family, and let them know you are still the same person even though you have dementia and may have behavioural changes over time.

There are many things we can do in our churches to help to support the person who is experiencing dementia symptoms. One of the most effective methods is the use of a memory box, which helps initiate communication by encouraging the person to speak about the objects in the box.[3] Objects that can be placed in the box include, for example, pictures of the person with others such as their children or other members of the church; articles such as gifts that the person was given a few years ago; and postcards that have been sent to the person from a friend. The memory box could help to bring back happy memories especially when the person remembers the story behind a particular gift or picture found in it.

In the church, using a memory box can help in case of an altercation taking place with a person who is experiencing difficulty remembering where they are and feeling muddled. It can help to distract and calm them and de-escalate the situation. Discussing meaningful objects placed in the memory box can help sharpen long-term memory. For instance, we could talk to them and have them talk to us about pictures that were taken many years ago. I would recommend consent be sought from the pastor, the person with dementia symptoms or their family prior to starting the process of making a memory box.

For the churches and families who have someone experiencing the symptoms, there are various websites available that can serve as valuable resources, such as:

- The Alzheimer's Society
- Dementia UK
- NICE Guidelines
- The World Health Organisation

Some of the activities that the church can provide to support those with dementia and their families include:

- Coffee mornings: hosting casual meetings over coffee where we offer classes on various activities and crafts including knitting and cooking, provide advice on healthy eating and helpful information on dementia care, undertake blood pressure monitoring and more.
- Convocations: attending annual meetings where all our churches gather for worship services and various workshops for our spiritual, physical and medical needs.
- Talks at different church locations: giving speeches where the speakers provide invaluable advice on dementia management and share personal testimonies. We have already given presentations at a few churches including our national headquarters in Birmingham and have received excellent feedback.

In addition, listed below are precautionary steps to foster a safe and supportive environment for dementia patients both at home and at church, as recommended by Alzheimer's Society, Dementia UK, and NICE Guidelines[4,5,6]:

- Removing rugs can help prevent elderly people from mistaking them for puddles of water that they have to jump

over, which poses a fall/trip hazard potentially leading to an injury to hips/knees.
- Covering mirrors can help because people with dementia may not recognize themselves in the mirror and feel confused.
- Beware of laminate flooring; some of our Treasured Saints wearing hearing aids due to sight and hearing loss can be alarmed by amplified footsteps due to the material.
- Soundproofing places with carpets and cushions helps absorb sound, which in turn could help the person whose hearing is not as it used to be. Soft furnishings improve sound absorption by reducing the volume of sounds heard around the room and also enhance sound quality for those using hearing aids.
- Putting labels on cupboards in the kitchen—such as where knives, forks, cups and plates are—can aid those who can't remember where these tools are kept.
- Installing motion sensor lights at church or at home can help prevent falls and also reduce confusion as both the elderly with sight impairment and those with dementia would benefit from not having to search for the light switch.
- Keeping the curtains open and removing unnecessary nets/blinds would increase natural light and allow those with sight concerns to see more clearly.
- Using clocks with LCD may help to see numbers more clearly and to remember the correct time and date that those with dementia may have difficulty figuring out.

- Using telephones with large buttons can help them call a family member if needed; placing the numbers of friends and family by the phone would also be of great help.
- Senior-proofing tables, ensuring that the edges are round, can prevent injuries.
- Ensuring that the safety measures are in good working order can help prevent accidents: e.g., fences and gates to prevent those with dementia from wandering off.
- Making notes of useful information can be helpful; for instance, write down where the remote control is usually kept so that it can be easily located.

Another great resource is the LifeBook, a booklet distributed by Age UK as a free resource. It has helped our Treasured Saints to have it filled out and kept in place so that they have all the necessary information pertaining to the later stage of their lives documented together in case of an emergency, which includes their personal details, contacts, finances, insurance policies, possessions and final wishes. Our elderly members have expressed their gratitude for having this resource available, as this comprehensive document allows them to take many important aspects of their lives into consideration while they have the capacity to do so. End-of-life planning, as you will learn further in later chapters, is a crucial step that must not be overlooked.

The following are additional ways in which we can help our brethren with dementia, as advised by Alzheimer's Society and Dementia UK[4,5]:

- Offer help with everyday tasks, such as gardening, shopping and laying the table at home before mealtimes, which would help them maintain their skills.

- Speak clearly and allow them some time to respond; they may be overwhelmed with feelings, which would make them slower to respond.
- Give them simple questions or choices that they can easily answer or choose from and refraining from overwhelming them with too many choices.
- Remember to always include them in conversations without ridiculing them or putting them under pressure.
- Be patient with them at all times as they may repeat themselves or struggle to find the right word.

Remember that it is not the person's fault that they are unwell. The Bible teaches us in Proverbs 15:1, "A soft answer turneth away wrath but grievous words stir up anger"; and in Colossians 4:6, "Let your speech be always with grace, seasoned with salt, that ye may know how ye ought to answer every man." We must live by these words and show kindness and patience even when they lash out physically and verbally. As our beloved Bishop M H Simmonds would say, "Let our words be sweet you may have to eat them." Speak gently and kindly at all times to our brethren experiencing these symptoms that are beyond their control. We must put ourselves in their shoes, have empathy and try to understand how difficult it must be for them to no longer have control over their impulses.

When an altercation breaks out, maintain your composure. Pastor R Bell would advise that we pour a bucket of cold water on the situation if a person is getting too upset; in other words, we must avoid adding to the fumes of the fire but calm it down. Ushers and Deacons can be called upon when an altercation is taking place, and they will intervene and try to sort out the conflict caused by the person experiencing one of the following symptoms that accompany dementia[8,9]:

- Delusions: beliefs that are not based on reality
- Hallucinations: hearing/seeing things that do not exist

Here are some helpful exercises that we can do to de-escalate altercations in the church:

- Counting to 10, which will give us some time to think and figure out the best response
- Taking a deep breath in through the nose and out through the mouth, which will help us relax and take our minds off the conflict

Other ways of helping our Treasured Saints and anyone with early onset dementia include:

- Undertaking the Lord's supper in the safety and convenience of their homes or their current residences such as a home for the elderly
- Scheduling home visits or Zoom meetings to enable them to participate in the Bible study and church service without leaving their homes and to check up on them on a regular basis to ensure that they are doing well and are not feeling alone
- Arranging group activities in their homes, such as knitting, sewing and listening to music together, to help them feel less isolated

Above all, let us live by Galatians 5:22 which preaches the fruit of the Spirit:

- Love
- Joy
- Peace

- Longsuffering
- Gentleness
- Goodness
- Faith
- Meekness
- Temperance

Some words of encouragement from the Holy Bible:

- Proverbs 18:21 declares that death and life are in the power of the tongue—let us speak life, not death, to one another.
- We do not want any illness at all but if they occur 1 Peter 5:7 tells us to cast all our cares on Jesus for he cares for us.
- Philippians 4:8 reminds us to think on whatever is true, honest, just, pure, lovely and of good report —anything of virtue and deserving of praise.
- Proverbs 23:7 says, "For as a man thinketh in his heart, so is he." We should always try to think positively about ourselves.

REFERENCES

1. Dementia. World Health Organization. Published August 8, 2019. Accessed July 2023. https://www.who.int/health-topics/dementia#tab=tab_1
2. Clinical Features - Diagnosis - Dementia. NICE Guidelines. Published 2022. Accessed 2023. https://cks.nice.org.uk/topics/dementia/diagnosis/clinical-features/
3. Memory Box. Alzheimer's Society. Accessed July 2023. https://shop.alzheimers.org.uk/collections/help-around-the-home/products/memory-box?variant=42366933336218
4. Making your home dementia friendly. Alzheimer's Society. Published October 2015. Accessed July 2023. https://www.alzheimers.org.uk/sites/default/files/migrate/downloads/making_your_home_dementia_friendly.pdf
5. Making the home safe and comfortable for a person with dementia. Dementia UK. https://www.dementiauk.org/information-and-support/living-with-dementia/making-the-home-safe-and-comfortable-for-a-person-with-dementia/
6. Scenario: Management in primary care - Hearing loss in adults. NICE Guidelines. Published 2019. Accessed 2023. https://cks.nice.org.uk/topics/hearing-loss-in-adults/management/management-in-primary-care/#hearing-aids-assistive-listening-devices
7. Lifebook. Age UK. Accessed July 2023. https://www.ageuk.org.uk/information-advice/money-legal/end-of-life-planning/lifebook/

8. Dementia Symptoms. Alzheimer's Society. Accessed July 2023. https://www.alzheimers.org.uk/about-dementia/symptoms-and-diagnosis/dementia-symptoms
9. Delusions, paranoia and dementia. Alzheimer's Society. Accessed July 2023. https://www.alzheimers.org.uk/about-dementia/symptoms-and-diagnosis/delusions

CHAPTER 4:

CARING FOR THE CARER

MRS DEZRENE JONES-BEEZER

CARING FOR SOMEONE LIVING WITH DEMENTIA

The definition of a carer is a family member or paid helper who regularly looks after a child or a sick, elderly or disabled person. As much as the elderly people that they look after, the carers need long-term support that extends beyond their time spent doing their jobs.

When someone close to you is diagnosed with dementia, you, the carer, need support; it is likely your first time taking on the responsibility to take care of someone who is unable to take care of themselves. It can be difficult to know which way to turn and daunting to find yourself suddenly described as a *carer*. Yesterday you were a family member free of the heavy burden now pressing down on your shoulders.

THE CARING ROLE

The overall caring role can be very challenging both to the carer and the individual diagnosed with dementia. From the onset of the diagnosis and throughout the changes and challenges whilst caring, you as the carer will need support at some point, especially when you don't have any other family members who can help or take over and give you a break.

Less support leads to more stress, depression, or anxiety, sleep deprivation and fatigue from spending long hours caring and not getting enough breaks. You may find yourself struggling to prioritise your physical health and struggling to balance other commitments. You may experience difficulty maintaining relationships with friends and family and coping with behaviours from the patients that require endless patience.

As a carer you must be made aware that dementia changes from one stage to another; the patient may experience no memory deficit initially and proceed to severe dementia. Whilst caring for your loved ones, you may notice the challenges growing severe over time. You will have to make difficult, uncomfortable decisions and strive to keep a sound mind along the way. Once your needs have been assessed, professional actions should be considered, depending on the severity of dementia of the patient that you are caring for, which may lead to having to care for them in a resident care setting like care homes.

Even though caring for the person living with dementia is undoubtedly difficult for anyone, it is the Lord's desire for you to maintain your composure and control over your own mind. The Lord has given us wisdom to use; if you are overwhelmed by these challenges as a carer, you can reach out to professionals like the GP, dementia nurses and social workers to utilise their expertise and judgement.

"For God hath not given us the spirit of fear; but of power, and of love, and of a sound mind." (11 Timothy 1:7)

"Thou wilt keep him in perfect peace whose mind is stayed on thee: because he trusts in thee." (Isaiah 26:3)

AVAILABLE SUPPORT FOR CARERS

- Please ensure you're registered as a carer with your General Practitioner (GP).
- Please ensure you complete a Carer's Assessment. You can ask the local council social worker or go onto the website gov.uk.

Carer's Assessment is free and available for anyone over 18. Once you have completed the assessment, the result might show you recommendations catered to your situation, such as having someone to take over your responsibility as a carer so you can have a break, training how to lift safely, getting help with housework, shopping and/or getting in touch with local support groups and finding people to talk to.

RESOURCES FOR ADDITIONAL SUPPORT

- Training courses for carers
- Local support groups on the Alzheimer's Society Website
- Carers' groups (where carers can share similar experiences)
- Adaptation to Home (applying equipment's, changes such as walk in shower etc)
- Technology lifeline (for the person living with Dementia); this may help to alleviate some of your anxieties as the carer
- Access to Day Centre and lunch clubs

PRACTICAL TIPS

- Be realistic and kind to yourself
- Set your priorities
- Know that you cannot do everything on your own and won't be able to please everyone
- Talk about your emotions
- Ask for help when needed
- Take respite so that you are not overburdening yourself

The Lord's desire is not for you to suffer in silence but rather to lighten your burden.

"Finally, brethren, whatsoever things are true, whatsoever things are honest, whatsoever things are just, whatsoever things are pure, whatsoever things are lovely, whatsoever things are of good report; if there be any virtue, and if there be any praise, think on these things." (Philippians 4:8)

DEMENTIA AND OTHER COMORBIDITIES MAY LEAD TO HOSPITAL ADMISSIONS

As a carer you may start having anxieties about what would happen next as your family member is admitted into hospital. You may start thinking you will never see them again or the worse might happen.

Having dementia and other comorbidities may lead to hospital admission as in the case of 86-year-old Dr John Gerrard who was diagnosed with Alzheimer's disease. His family could no longer care for him at home due to an infected leg ulcer not responding to antibiotics. This led to a hospital admission at the start of January 2014. The hospital then had a norovirus outbreak, which meant no visitors were allowed. During John's hospital stay, visits from his family were severely restricted. John was discharged home, but his conditions deteriorated, and he ultimately passed away in November 2014. In the wake of his death, John's daughter, Nicci Gerrard, co-founded John's Campaign.

John's Campaign is the right of relatives or carers to stay with people with dementia in hospitals outside of visiting times, which applies to all hospital settings and some care homes. As a carer you can make enquiries from the hospital to which your relative is admitted.

REASONS TO SUPPORT JOHN'S CAMPAIGN

Compassion: People with dementia are confused and can be frightened of people. A hospital stay can be unnerving for anyone at any age; dementia patients find it difficult to cope with being in hospital, so it helps immensely to have a family member, a friend, a neighbour, a known carer or any other familiar faces that they trust.

Care: Involving a family carer from the moment of the patient's admission to hospital until the moment of discharge has been proven to ensure a higher quality of care and improved chances of positive outcomes. Having extended visiting rights means carers of patients with dementia, whose presence has numerous benefits, are welcome at any time. Since the COVID 19 outbreak, the John's Campaign is not consistently embraced in hospitals.

I am currently pursuing a Development Leadership Aspirant Course facilitated by NHS England, which entails a stretch assignment on a project that can be implemented in my current hospital with the potential to take it to other hospitals as well. I have relaunched John's Campaign with the goal of alleviating relatives' or carers' anxieties when family members are admitted to hospitals away from their usual environment.

Once you have made it through all, the Lord will reward you greatly.

"For God is not unrighteous to forget your work and labour of love, which ye have shewed towards his name, in that ye have ministered to the saints, and do minister. And we desire that every one of you do shew the same diligence to the full assurance of hope unto the end. That ye be not slothful, but followers of them who through faith and patience inherit the promises." (Hebrews 6:10-12)

REFERENCES AND RESOURCES FOR FURTHER HELP

1. Admiral Nurse Dementia Helpline: 0800 888 6678
2. Age UK National Helpline: 0800 678 1602
3. Alzheimer's Society Publication
4. Carers Direct (helpline for carers): 0300 123 1053
5. Carers UK
6. *Caring for a person with dementia: A practical guide*: free to download on the Alzheimer's Society website or order by post
7. Dementia UK Helpline (open 9am to 9pm weekdays): helpline@dementiauk.org

HOW DO I GET IN TOUCH WITH JOHN'S CAMPAIGN?

To get in touch, please email Julia Jones (julia-jones@talk21.com) or Nicci Gerrard (nicci.gerrard@icloud.com). Julia can also be reached by phone at 01245 231898.

You can follow John's Campaign on Facebook and on https://johnscampaign.org.uk.

CHAPTER 5:

THE LAW AND DEMENTIA

MR DANIEL SIMMONDS

In all aspects of life, the law of the land gives people a sense of security, boundaries and recourse, which is particularly the case for people with dementia.

It'd be impossible to fully discuss the complexities of the law or the various ways that it affects or interacts with the lives of dementia patients within these pages. However, I will aim to provide you with sufficient information about two particular documents which suddenly become important when someone is diagnosed with dementia.

Without further ado, the two documents I'd like to discuss are:
- A Lasting Power of Attorney
- A Last Will and Testament

LASTING POWER OF ATTORNEY (LPA)

There are two types of LPA: the first concerns health and welfare, the second property and financial affairs.

WHAT IS AN LPA?

An LPA is a document that allows you (the donor) to appoint one or more people (attorneys) to help you make decisions or make decisions on your behalf, which gives you more control over what happens to you if you have an accident or illness (e.g., dementia) and are physically or mentally unfit to make decisions at any given point.[1] It is then paramount that you select attorneys that you trust, whether they are family members or friends.

HOW TO MAKE AN LPA

First of all, think about who you can trust with your health and welfare and/or your hard-earned cash and investments. You may find, after reading this guide, that your circle reduces significantly in size. You'd be better off choosing a Jonathan over a Saul (1 Sam 18:1). Steer clear of those who don't understand how to manage their own finances because they'll be worse with yours.

Secondly, locate and complete the necessary form(s) on gov.uk and register these completed forms with the Office of the Public Guardian. Should you complete these forms by yourself, it will come at a sum of £82 per form; there are two forms to be filled out, the property and financial form and the health and welfare form, therefore equalling £164. However, if you seek help from a legal professional, it may cost you more.

WHEN IS THE RIGHT TIME TO SET UP AN LPA?

The best time to set up an LPA is *as soon as you*'ve finished *reading this chapter*. With the information that you now have from reading this guide, do so as soon as possible—what you don't want to do is to wait until you've been diagnosed with a condition like dementia because then your mental capacity is brought into question. Spare yourself the headache and set up your LPA *whilst* you have your faculties.

What happens if my parents/close relative is starting to lose or have lost their faculties and there is no LPA in place?

A 'deputyship' application can be made to the Court of Protection. This court specifically looks after individuals who can no longer make their own decisions. Successful deputyship applications enable relatives or friends to be appointed as the person's decision-maker, or deputy.[2]

The Court can appoint two different types of deputies: one to make decisions about the individual's personal welfare and one to manage their property and affairs.

In most cases, the Court appoints a deputy to make decisions on matters involving property and affairs. The appointed deputy then would be expected to decide on the individual's care home fees or property refurbishments as necessary.[3] It must be noted that the precise responsibility and powers of a deputy are specified in the Court of Protection order appointing them.[4]

As a general rule, however, do *not* wait until it is left up to a court to decide who should be making decisions about you and for you. The court may inadvertently pick someone who doesn't wish you well, in which case you'll either have no recourse or find it hard to argue your case. Complete your LPAs *now*, whether you're 35, 55 or 65.

Now let's move on to another very important document, which most of you readers have probably heard about already. You guessed it right—the will.

WHAT IS A WILL?

Leaving an inheritance is a biblical principle. King Solomon wrote, "A good man leaveth an inheritance to his children's children; and the wealth of the sinner is laid up for the just" (Proverbs 13:22). A will is a legal document that has been written and executed by a testator expressing their wishes in relation to the dividing of their estate. In simpler terms, a will is a legal document which sets out who gets what when someone dies. Or in some cases, who doesn't get anything. I know which side I'd rather be on.

WHAT MAKES A WILL LEGAL?

Or rather what makes a will *binding?* I'm glad you asked! Let's take a closer look at the criteria that need to be satisfied:

- It must be in writing, signed by you and witnessed by two people (who should not be your spouse, children or anyone that you want to place on the will; otherwise they will not receive anything under the will).
- You must have the mental capacity to make the will and understand the effect that it will have.
- You must make the will voluntarily and without pressure from anyone else.[5]
- You must be 18 years old or over at the time of writing your will.

If the above requirements are not met, you will have an invalid will, which makes the entire process unnecessarily complicated and upsetting for all those involved.

CAN A PERSON WITH DEMENTIA MAKE A VALID WILL?

By now you are probably trying to answer this question yourself. If you are, good for you; it helps to ponder these questions as we go. Write your answer down on a piece of paper and test yourself. Yes? No? It depends?

The correct answer is: *it depends*. If a person has dementia, in order for their will to be valid, their dementia must not affect their ability to make decisions about the will.[6]

HOW DO I GO ABOUT MAKING A WILL?

You can write it yourself, provided that you comply with all of the requirements. If you're unsure whether your will would be deemed valid after you have passed away, you can feel free to consult a solicitor. Other alternatives would be talking to your bank or even the Co-op.

HOW MUCH DOES IT COST?

That depends on how simple or complex your will would be.

If you look into your bank account and, like me, believe your will would be very simple, it'd probably cost you between £150 and £250. However, if there are more zeros in your account balance before the decimal point, and if you own multiple houses, land, money overseas and trusts, then that could cost you up to £600 and beyond. Remember to read the terms and conditions when anybody is selling you a will-writing service, as there may be other hidden fees involved, such as storage fees. So, please do your due diligence, and don't feel pressured to hand over any money to these service providers until you know exactly what you are signing up for.

WHAT HAPPENS IF THERE IS NO WILL?

Please do *not* take this chance because the ramifications are far reaching. If there is no will, then the estate will be distributed as if the deceased had never made a will according to the rules of intestacy,[7] which are a body of statutory laws that determine how your estate is to be divided. The law, in this instance, will try to find your closest surviving relative(s), starting from your spouse, then moving on to your children and so on. Should you not have any immediate family members or relatives, all of your hard-earned money will go to the Crown. Bear in mind you have supported the Crown all of your working life through your taxes; I wouldn't exactly recommend that you pay them even when you die.

To wrap up, these are what I'd like you to take away from this chapter:
- An LPA is effective up until the point you die; it has no effect afterwards.
- Your will comes into play once you have died, effective immediately.
- Please do not wait until you lack the mental capacity to think about making an LPA or drafting a will. Do it *now*.

Please know that what I have explained so far in this chapter is not meant to be legal advice, but merely a series of guidelines to help you make your own decisions or to find the right people to consult. If you are in any doubt, there are a number of resources you can refer to and people you can talk to, starting with:
- a wills and probate lawyer

   and/or
- the Citizens Advice Bureau

REFERENCES

1. Make, register or end a lasting power of attorney. GOV.UK. Published December 2, 2011. Accessed July 2023. https://www.gov.uk/power-of-attorney
2. What happens if my parent develops dementia and there is no lasting power of attorney? WHN Solicitors. Published September 2, 2017. Accessed July 2023. https://www.whnsolicitors.co.uk/newsroom/individuals/dementia-no-last-power-attorney/
3. Deputies - legal information. MIND. Published April 2023. Accessed July 17, 2023. https://www.mind.org.uk/information-support/legal-rights/mental-capacity-act-2005/deputies/
4. The Court of Protection and the Appointment of a Deputy. Becket Chambers. 3 July 2020. Accessed July 2023. https://becket-chambers.co.uk/2020/07/03/the-court-of-protection-and-the-appointment-of-a-deputy/#:~:text=The%20precise%20responsibility%20and%20powers%20of%20a%20deputy,deal%20with%20broader%20decisions%20on%20an%20ongoing%20basis.
5. Making a will - all you need to know. Age UK. Accessed July 2023. https://www.ageuk.org.uk/information-advice/money-legal/legal-issues/making-a-will/#:~:text=For%20a%20will%20to%20be
6. Can someone with dementia make a will? Alzheimer's Society. Accessed July 2023. https://www.alzheimers.org.uk/get-support/publications-and-factsheets/dementia-together-magazine/can-someone-dementia-make-will
7. Who can inherit if there is no will – the rules of intestacy. Citizens Advice. Published 2019. Accessed July 2023. https://www.citizensadvice.org.uk/family/death-and-wills/who-can-inherit-if-there-is-no-will-the-rules-of-intestacy/

CHAPTER 6A:

LIVING WITH SOMEONE WITH DEMENTIA

↯

MRS ELENE MAYNARD-SCANTLEBURY

My story started quite abruptly in 2019 when I received a call from the police who told me that my mother was having a nervous breakdown because someone had broken into her house and stolen her medication.

My mother had given them my contact information when asked about family, which had led to them contacting me in the middle of the night. At that time my mother lived in Reading, Berkshire, and I lived in Birmingham, so I could not be there right away. The police had a brief chat with me about my mother over the phone and contacted her General Practitioner (GP) to arrange an appointment for the following morning. My son and I went to Reading the next day and took her to the appointment. She was given a preliminary memory test, and her blood pressure was also taken. We discussed her general wellbeing with the doctor.

As we were leaving the consultation room, the doctor called me back and informed me that my mother had failed the memory test and that they would be contacting the psychiatric team at the hospital. The psychiatric nurses visited her at home two weeks later. An assessment procedure was carried out; they explained to my mother why they were conducting the assessment and then the same to me. They told us before leaving that they would do a report, which I received two weeks later. My mother was diagnosed with mixed dementia.

I had to move to Reading where a CPN (Community Psychiatric Nurse) was assigned to my mother. While living with her, I saw a side of her created by dementia that I had never thought I'd see: she was constantly paranoid about imaginary squatters living in her loft and also strongly convinced that they were stealing her food and cooking it under her roof. Although at this stage she could still carry out basic chores for herself (e.g., washing, cooking and cleaning), I noticed that she was not able to do them as well as when she had been well. As weeks went by, more health issues came on board, such as arthritis in the spine and knees and secondary cancer.

My mother was in total denial. I tried to explain to her that she had been diagnosed with dementia because by this time she had entered the middle stages. She would accuse me of stealing her money and moving items that she had put in particular places without her permission, which I would vehemently deny. While cleaning and organising her things, I would find neglected bills and reminders in the airing cupboard under the bed linen and her handbag in the fridge or the oven. She started to lose interest in her favourite television programmes; sometimes she would say she was going to watch TV but then do something different, having completely forgotten her original plan.

As her dementia progressed, I could see her decision-making capacity declining and agitation becoming increasingly common. I found it difficult to cope with the situation because sometimes the person I saw was 'not my mother'. She would barricade herself in her bedroom by moving a triple wardrobe, a dressing table and armchair to bolt the door. She would hide fruit, rice and biscuits in the bed drawers and the ottoman, thinking she was hiding them from the squatters who would otherwise steal them from her. It was hard for me to comprehend, so I reached out to social services who came and performed an assessment on my mother. They looked around the house for anything that might inconvenience her daily and said they would provide assistance in finding the solutions, such as raising the chair she struggled to get out of and installing a shower stool and toilet rail. Upon leaving they said that I'd hear from them on completion of the report.

Four weeks later I still hadn't heard anything so I decided to reach back out to them. The Duty Social Worker informed me that because they did not deem her a danger to herself, my mum's case had already been closed, of which I was completely unaware. At this point I was crying. After hanging up, I contacted the CPN at the psychiatric hospital and told her that social services had closed my mother's case. The CPN let me know that the hospital had received a letter informing them of the situation and that she would arrange a visit to come and see us. I couldn't help but feel that the professionals who were supposed to safeguard my mum in her situation had let us down. Whoever I reached out to didn't seem to want to know; even the CPN did her bare minimum.

As time passed my mother's dementia took a toll on me. I had more and more difficulty dealing with my mom's outbursts and her unflinching belief that the squatters were real. When I took her out shopping, she would repeat to everyone she met the same story of squatters living in her house. She was calling out the names of those who were not in the room or even those who had already passed on. My sleep pattern was broken because she had lost her sense of time and would go to bed at 4 p.m. and wake up at 3 a.m. She often played 'musical beds', meaning she would go to sleep in one room and wake up in another, as she was convinced that someone was watching her while she slept. Little by little I saw her memory diminish; even cooking had become a problem and I had to help with her day-to-day living. The hardest part for me was helping her with her personal care because she would deny that she needed my help. I was constantly on edge, trying to mentally visualise what trouble she might be getting into at any given time.

On occasions, when I had to travel back to Birmingham, a neighbour would step in and make sure she took her medication. Despite their help I knew that my phone would be buzzing with calls from the police as soon as I arrived. At one point the police called and said that my mother had gone to a shop where the shopkeeper was familiar with her and had told another patron of the shop about the squatters in her house, so they had taken her to the police station. Since the police had her condition on record, they assured me that they had dispatched two officers to the house and another to take her home after checking the entire house to make sure that no one was there. Mum never believed them.

From that point, it only became worse and got to the point where I couldn't travel to Birmingham as often. She would not pick up when I called her, and I would then have to phone the neighbour to check on her. I installed surveillance cameras for peace of mind; it also enabled me to see where she was hiding various items. As my mum needed more help from me, I reached out to the CPN asking what my options were, to which she responded, "I can't tell you what to do with your mom. She's your mom and you need to decide what to do with her." The nurse advised that I take a look at the directory of care homes that she would send me.

My mother's memory was deteriorating right in front of me; she was forgetting people's names including mine. She was hardly doing any household chores and would hide her clothes and throw them in the bin. She started to destroy anything within her reach to pieces, thinking that she was fixing it even though it didn't need any fixing. She also had sleep problems, for which her GP prescribed her sleeping tablets. Shopping became a rarer occurrence because she wanted to venture outdoors less and less and because she had arthritic knees and walked much slower than before. Whenever she did want to go out, she would never have sufficient money for what she wanted, having forgotten to bring it with her, so I'd end up paying for everything. By December my mother was on quite a lot of medication for paranoia, sleep disorders, high blood pressure and arthritic pain.

By this time my own mental health had started to decline, so I decided to ask my mother's neighbour if she could keep an eye on her for just a couple of days whilst I returned to Birmingham. When I finally arrived back in my own home, I reached out to Dementia UK and Alzheimer's Society for advice and then to care homes in Birmingham. After getting all the advice and information I needed and finding out how easy it would be to get my mother to Birmingham, I made the decision and found a home that would admit her. I went back to Reading and contacted her CPN and told her that I had found a home for my mother and that I'd need her file to be faxed directly to them. I also informed the GP that I was moving my mother to Birmingham.

Within two weeks we had relocated my mother to a care home in Birmingham. Until then I had not realised how much of an impact my mother's dementia had had on my mental state. It would be an understatement to say that seeing my mother die a little bit each day while having to maintain a distance from her to deal with the instances of aggression and agitation was hard to accept; it was as if pieces of myself were being torn away from me every waking moment.

My mother stayed in that particular nursing home for around five months, but as she deteriorated she needed more intensive one-to-one care. The care home decided that we needed to find her a new home that would better accommodate her needs. To complicate it even further, this change was happening during COVID-19, which brought on more stress as I was not allowed to visit my mother. I could speak to her via phone call, but because she did not have the capacity to hold a conversation, she wouldn't respond or speak to me after saying hello. It hurt a lot knowing that I was losing my mum and being left in the dark as to how long it would be before I could see her in person or as to whether she would even recognise me the next time we saw each other.

Even after the home started window visits, my mother did not want to see us most of the time. The hardest time was in late January 2021 when I received a call from the home that my mum had tested positive for COVID. The next two days I was at my wits' end. I was on tender hooks every time the phone rang, wondering what they would be telling me next.

Four days later I got a call around lunchtime from the head nurse who told me that my mother was doing poorly and that they would continue to keep me updated. Within three hours the nurse called back to ask me how long it would take me to get to the home from then. I immediately got a lift to the home where a staff member was waiting for me; they ushered me to a room to put on PP equipment and then took me to my mother's room where she was lying unresponsive. I could not stop crying as I stroked her cheeks, calling her name, but no matter what I did, she still showed no response. After twenty minutes of being alone with my mother, I started to think: *this is it*.

When I came out of the room, the head nurse asked me to follow her into another room where she wanted to discuss the End of Life Care for my mother, the concept of which, at the time, I found hard to grasp. She explained that it was something I had to do in case my mother took a turn for the worst. I put one in place as advised and left.

On my way home I reached out to my church prayer group, told them the situation and asked them to pray for my mother. After two days she was still with us—God had answered our prayers.

My mother eventually overcame COVID, but as she was still in a care home, it opened up a whole slew of problems that Afro-Caribbean people face in homes with personal care and diet. I put my best efforts to keep my mother feeling comfortable as if she were in her own home and as if she didn't have dementia. Diet and hygiene played vital roles to maintain that sense of normalcy. For instance, keeping her on a diet with food that she would recognise she used to eat before she had lost her memory immensely helped, but the home in which she resided unfortunately did not provide a special diet that catered to Afro-Caribbeans, which meant she had to rely on her family to bring it in to keep her in her culture. Apart from the culture-specific issues, clothing posed another complication: new clothes bought for her were ripped within four weeks even though my mother was not mobile, with holes developing on pieces that had not been worn more than once. I decided to bring her laundry home and take care of it myself.

Other problems warranted more serious concerns. I had a call on a Thursday evening at around 7 p.m. from the head nurse who said there was something wrong with the right side of my mother's body. I was not provided with a clear explanation over the phone as to what the issue exactly was. When my son and I went in the following day, the head nurse walked us to the lounge where my mother was sitting. I nearly fell over when I saw a wound on the right side of my mother's face. Seeing that my son and I were both in shock upon seeing the wound, the nurse gestured towards us to follow her into another room. There she explained that she had gone into my mother's room the day before and seen the right side of her face pushed against the wall with her right arm hanging over the edge of the bed towards the floor in her sleep. The nurse had notified the deputy manager who identified that my mother had rolled herself towards the wall in her sleep, which had caused a visible surface injury to the right side of her face due to friction.

The nurse could not tell us when this accident had happened. My son and I asked for the day-to-day report, a copy of the incident log and a proper meeting in my mother's room to discuss what had exactly taken place. During the meeting I asked if I could demonstrate to prove that it was impossible for my mum to have obtained such a serious facial injury as described in their report. My mother's bed was pushed to the wall, so if I positioned myself on the bed on my right side as my mom would have lain, it would be impossible for her to get into the position that they had allegedly seen her in. They continued to stick to their story even though they couldn't prove it, nor could they tell us how my mother had gotten her face injured due to the lack of any record on the Hourly Report Sheet regarding the incident; I felt that they were showing no genuine concern for her. After the meeting I left feeling disheartened and trampled on—I felt that I had let my mum down. I did report the incident to CQC (Commission Quality Care) and Social Services Safeguarding.

There were, however, moments that truly warmed my heart towards my mother's last days. Starting in August, her health started to decline even further. The staff at the home ensured that she was cared for at a level that I had not witnessed before, maximising her comfort and sense of safety during her last weeks. They demonstrated both care and compassion as they attended to her every need. An in-depth conversation with the doctor, a crucial part of dementia care, ensured that adequate pain management was administered, as I emphasised her wish to be free from pain in her final moments.

On August 17 my mom's eating habits began to change, which meant caring for her became even more challenging. The dedicated staff allowed me to be with her at all times, as it was imperative that I monitor her diet to make sure that her nutritional needs were met. In the last two weeks of her life, the care provided, especially by her assigned nurses and carers, exceeded expectations. They went above and beyond, even coming in on their days off duty, showing a level of care that touched me deeply. Her final night with us was an especially moving one: everyone at the home, from the head of the home to the cleaners, gathered to say goodbye to her.

On the morning of her passing, even the carers and nurses who were off duty that day came in and formed a guard of honour from her room on the ground floor to the front door as they took her away. In that moment, all I saw was love; I cried. Once she was gone, they paid their condolences, hugged me and wished me all the best. I am beyond grateful to the staff who made her last weeks as comfortable as possible.

On September 7, my mother thus left us, and I knew God had called her to a better place.

I had done my best for my mother. I had the honour and privilege of being there by her side until the end, which some families unfortunately do not get to have—an issue that must be resolved through our collective endeavours to support them in any way we can so that they have access to appropriate resources to provide the best possible care for their loved ones.

My experience in dementia care has led me down a new path where I have become an ambassador for Dementia UK. Based on my interactions with the professionals that weren't always positive, I decided I wanted to use my experience for the benefit of other families, especially Afro-Caribbeans, giving them access to all the helpful resources that I have gathered. I run a dementia clinic on Wednesdays for dementia carers. In addition, the manager of the care home where my mum passed away has requested that I start a similar support group for dementia carers at the home in the new year. I am also grateful to be working with the co-authors of this book, an amazing team of nurses, a doctor and a solicitor, who have provided such insightful talks on dementia.

With that all said, I implore that you, the reader, take my account with this disclaimer: the chapter you have read has been written solely based on my personal experience, which may not coincide with others' that are more positive in terms of their success with various organisations and support systems in place. Your own experience may turn out to be entirely different from mine. It is by no means my intention to claim that my story provides a full picture of dementia care, but only to present an honest account that is as comprehensive and as true to my lived experience as possible.

As my chapter comes to a tentative conclusion with the promise of new chapters ahead, I hope that you, too, take a moment to consider these action points:

- Initiate a support group for dementia awareness in the black community.

- Reach out to organisations and churches to collaborate on dementia education.
- Offer prayers and support for families dealing with dementia.
- Advocate for improved dementia care to ensure consistent quality care from the beginning to the end of one's journey.
- Share personal experiences to inform communities and reduce stigma around dementia.

I have parted with my mother, and the curtains have finally been drawn on the part of my life as her carer, but my dementia journey remains ongoing. As an active supporter I will continue to share what I learn from personally engaging with countless others giving their best to do right by their loved ones diagnosed with dementia.

Our efforts to help improve the overall field of dementia care should always be a work in progress. In the end, what matters above all else is our determination to move onwards—to draw wisdom from our past and plan and hope for a brighter future in dementia care and awareness.

CHAPTER 6B:

LIVING WITH DEMENTIA — "CHANGES"

MRS JACQUELINE NICELY

"The Lord is my light and my salvation, whom shall I fear. The Lord is the strength of my life. Of whom shall I be afraid." (Psalms 27:1)

Picture the scene: the children, now adults, fly the nest, graduate from university and start on their career paths. Marriages are on the horizon, then grandchildren are on the way. Hugh and I see retirement just around the corner, arguably the empty nesters' dream. We plan and embrace the next exciting chapter of our lives—until our path takes an unexpected turn.

I first noticed a change in Hugh's behaviour when a spontaneous outburst took place at a supermarket. However, at the time, the situation de-escalated fast and didn't seem serious enough. I left it at that. With hindsight, perhaps I should have pressed on it further.

Around this time the children would often ask their father if he was okay. While we were all chatting, laughing and reminiscing at the dinner table, he would sometimes drift off into his own world, as though he were daydreaming, oblivious to his surroundings—a clear behavioural change from what we were accustomed to. He was usually fully engaged and high-spirited not only around his family and friends, but around people in general. We felt that something wasn't right, but he continuously assured us that nothing was wrong.

After much discussion and persuasion, we managed to convince him to see a doctor, to dispel our fears and concerns. Once all of these arrangements had been made, he seemed to open up to us far more; he finally revealed that he too wondered whether he was becoming ill because for some time he had lost the ability to fully focus, read and study. He spoke about times in the pulpit when he was unexpectedly and inexplicably unable to speak. Hugh had not shared these concerns with any of us before, hoping that normalcy would be restored over time.

Upon examination, we were given the doctor's referral to an Alzheimer's Assessment Centre. There, following face-to-face discussions, practical tests and an MRI scan, the diagnosis came: frontotemporal variant dementia (early onset Alzheimer's Disease) at the rather tender age of 59. It meant, in layman's terms, that the personality of a personable and charming man, father, husband, son, brother, minister and more was slowly set to disappear.

Hugh's mannerisms and personality have changed remarkably. He has far less control over his own emotions including sorrow, joy and rage. Even his palette has changed, now far simpler and less adventurous. Family, friends, facts, common phrases, metaphors and everyday items are gradually becoming and will one day become completely unfamiliar to him. He is now fonder of earlier stages of his life than of more recent times. Like others diagnosed with dementia, he may unintentionally hurt and insult those who are near and dear, but we recognise and understand that these aggressive behaviours are beyond his control.

Currently there is no cure for the condition; it is being slowed and controlled with medication, which in turn carries challenging side-effects. All we know for sure is that God is omnipotent and He can do the unthinkable if it is His will. To quote St Luke 1:37, "For with God, nothing shall be impossible." As a family we are working fervently to support one another and provide a safe and comfortable environment for Hugh. It has arguably brought us all even closer. As the old saying goes, "God moves in a mysterious way, His wonders to perform."

In the midst of it all, Hugh and I are still blessed and continue to give our gratitude to the Highest. We have two gorgeous granddaughters given to us by our two amazing children who, along with their respective spouses, can't be more attentive, patient, and supportive. We always have something to look forward to: a long walk, a day out, a weekend away or a family holiday. Hugh loves to play the drums in the church, which enlivens him; you can see his joy and zeal for worship. We are documenting our memories with Hugh before they start slipping away. We are cherishing our present moments and making precious memories, for we know time is short and that our days are numbered.

Hugh can no longer safely work or drive, so his days at home can be long and lonely. Group therapy sessions are available, a few of which we have tried, but they are usually attended by individuals who are much older than him. Having few people to talk to throughout the day often makes him feel isolated. Each day brings new challenges, which can be as simple as a cupboard door being left open, lights being left on or a tap being left running. We try to deal with these incidents patiently while keeping in mind that we will inevitably face greater ones in the near future.

For those of you who know him personally, taking a few seconds to greet Hugh after a service and reintroduce yourself would be of great help to him, as he may not remember you even though you did the same the week before. Simply put, giving the gift of time shows that you care, which would be appreciated by all of us.

Many of us hail from a culture where we don't talk about our business, so to speak. While this piece has been challenging to write and share, I hope that this candid insight will serve as a helpful resource for someone out there in the world, especially since we live in an era where dementia is sadly on the rise.

Minister Hugh Evans Nicely was raised in the church. The church is his life. Please keep Hugh and our family in your thoughts and prayers. And lastly, please continue to pray for one another—for we know the power of prayer.

May God bless us all,

Jacqueline Nicely
Lloyd Nicely
Meisha-Grace Brabham

CHAPTER 7:

RISK FACTORS, COMPLICATIONS, PROGNOSIS AND MANAGEMENT

DR CAROL S. IGHOFOSE

WHAT ARE THE RISK FACTORS FOR DEMENTIA?

Several risk factors contribute to the development of dementia. The strongest one is age, with older individuals being more susceptible.[1] Mild cognitive impairment (MCI) also increases the risk, as approximately one-third of people with MCI progress to dementia within three years.[2] Learning disabilities, especially in individuals with Down's syndrome, are associated with a higher probability of dementia.[3] Genetic factors play a role as well with mutations in genes like APP and PSEN1/2 linked to familial Alzheimer's disease.[4] Cardiovascular conditions, cerebrovascular disease and Parkinson's disease also increase the risk of dementia.[5,6,7] Modifiable risk factors—such as lower educational attainment, hypertension, hearing impairment, smoking, obesity, depression, physical inactivity, diabetes, low social engagement, alcohol consumption, traumatic brain injury and exposure to air pollution—also contribute to dementia risk.[8,9,10]

WHAT ARE THE COMPLICATIONS OF DEMENTIA?

Dementia brings forth a range of challenges that impact the patients as well as their families or carers. These challenges highlight the multilayered nature of dementia; the condition affects the patients, their support networks and society as a whole in various regards and therefore requires comprehensive support to address the complex needs that accompany the condition.

Disability and dependency are common outcomes of dementia, making it one of the leading causes of functional limitations in older adults worldwide.[11] The ability to perform everyday activities, such as shopping, personal hygiene and maintaining the home, may become compromised.[12] Complex care needs arise, including aggressive or otherwise challenging behaviour, restlessness, eating problems and incontinence.[13] Mobility issues contribute to the risk of falls and fractures.[12,14]

Dementia also takes a toll on social connections, often leading to isolation and loss of interest in previously enjoyed activities.[13] The emergence of behavioural and psychological symptoms of dementia (BPSD)—which encompass agitation, depression, repetitive questioning, aggression, sleep disturbances and others—further adds to the burden.[13,15,16] It is worth noting that more than 90% of individuals with dementia will experience BPSD, which is associated with increased mortality, morbidity, hospital admissions and the need for long-term care.[14,16,17] As a result, institutionalisation becomes a reality for many patients, as the loss of independence and the increase in care requirements often necessitate residential placements.[18] If or when the time comes, family members need not feel guilt and shame that they have failed their loved ones, as long as the decision was made in the best interest of the person afflicted by dementia.

The impact of dementia extends to the wellbeing of carers as well. Heavy responsibilities of caring for someone with dementia can lead to stress, depression, financial strain, social isolation and/or a reduced quality of life.[13,16] Financial hardships may arise when the person with dementia loses their job or when carers have to reduce their working hours or even leave employment to provide care, particularly in cases of young-onset dementia.[13,19,20] In fact, it is estimated that about two-thirds of the overall cost of dementia is borne by individuals with dementia and their families or carers.

The importance of 'caring for the carer' has been dealt with in an earlier chapter.

WHAT IS THE PROGNOSIS FOR DEMENTIA?

Unfortunately, there is currently no cure or treatment to stop the progression of dementia.

Dementia can be roughly divided into three stages (although the speed at which it progresses varies among individuals):

- In **the early stage**, which lasts about one to two years, the signs may go unnoticed. It begins gradually with symptoms like forgetfulness, difficulty communicating, losing track of time and struggling to make decisions.
- In **the middle stage**, lasting approximately two to five years, more noticeable limitations come onboard. Memory loss becomes more severe; communication becomes increasingly difficult; assistance is needed for personal care; and simple tasks like preparing food become challenging. Behavioural changes may also occur during this stage.
- In **the late stage**, which occurs after five years or more, individuals experience near-total dependence and immobility. Memory disturbances grow severe; physical features become more pronounced; awareness of time and place declines; the ability to understand their surroundings and recognize loved ones fails; and eating requires assistance.

Dementia is a leading cause of death, accounting for a significant percentage of deaths in both men and women. In England and Wales, 12.5% of deaths in 2019 were attributed to dementia and Alzheimer's disease.

The time from diagnosis to death varies considerably. People diagnosed in their late 60s to early 70s typically have a median lifespan of 7 to 10 years, while those diagnosed in their 90s have a median lifespan of around 3 years. Studies have shown that mortality rates in the first year after dementia diagnosis are more than three times higher than those without dementia. In terms of survival time after diagnosis, the average is about 4.1 years, with approximately 14 months in the moderate stage and 12 months in the severe stage. Interestingly, women tend to survive longer in the severe stage compared to men. Dementia can progress more rapidly following an episode of delirium, a condition characterised by sudden confusion and disorientation.

DIAGNOSIS AND MANAGEMENT OF DEMENTIA

How do doctors manage persons with suspected dementia? (These are the key considerations and are essential for you to be aware of.)

- Arrange admission for individuals with suspected dementia if: they exhibit severe disturbances requiring intervention to ensure their health and safety or the safety of others. In some cases, detention under the Mental Health Act (1983) may be necessary.
- Refer individuals to a specialist dementia diagnostic service if reversible causes of cognitive decline have been identified while dementia is still suspected.
- Refer individuals with learning disabilities with suspected dementia to a psychiatrist with expertise in assessing and treating mental health problems in these cases.

- Refer individuals who are suspected to have rapidly progressive dementia to a neurological service with access to relevant tests.

For individuals with mild cognitive impairment (MCI):
- Discuss the diagnosis without causing undue anxiety.
- Arrange regular follow-up visits to monitor cognitive deficit progression.
- Encourage healthy brain activities such as regular exercise, word games and socialisation.
- Discuss the regulations on driving and cognitive impairment set by the Driver and Vehicle Licensing Agency (DVLA).
- Treat any identified modifiable risk factors for cognitive impairment.

Specialist investigations for suspected dementia

Structural imaging, such as magnetic resonance imaging (MRI) or computed tomography (CT) scan, should be included as a specialist investigation.

Additional investigations may include:
- Fluorodeoxyglucose-positron emission tomography-CT (FDG-PET) or Perfusion SPECT (single-photon emission CT)
- I-FP-CIT SPECT for suspected dementia with Lewy bodies (DLB) or I-MIBG cardiac scintigraphy
- Cerebrospinal fluid examination from a lumbar tap, which can help exclude infection, inflammation or malignancy and make a positive diagnosis of Alzheimer's disease and prion disease

SPECIALIST MANAGEMENT FOR DEMENTIA

Non-pharmacological interventions for mild to moderate dementia may include:
- Cognitive stimulation therapy
- Group reminiscence therapy
- Cognitive rehabilitation or occupational therapy

Drug treatments for cognitive symptoms should be initiated by clinicians with expertise, and treatment may continue under a shared-care protocol between the hospital specialist and the patient/client's general practitioner (GP) or family doctor. Options include:
- Acetylcholinesterase (AChE) inhibitors (donepezil, galantamine and rivastigmine) for managing mild to moderate Alzheimer's disease.
- Memantine as monotherapy for managing moderate or severe Alzheimer's disease or in addition to AChE inhibitors.
- Treatment of non-Alzheimer's dementia with AChE inhibitors or memantine is unlicensed but may be prescribed by a specialist based on individual needs.
- Drug treatments for non-cognitive symptoms, such as antipsychotics, should only be initiated under specialist supervision.

Driving and Cognitive Impairment

For individuals with mild cognitive impairment, driving restrictions depend on the level of impairment and should be assessed by medical professionals according to DVLA regulations.

Individuals with dementia **must** notify the DVLA. Note that their driving licences may be revoked or subject to annual review.

How to Support a Person Diagnosed with Dementia

Receiving a diagnosis of dementia can be overwhelming for both the individual and their loved ones. To provide the best care and support, it is crucial to understand the necessary steps and considerations. Supporting a person with dementia requires a comprehensive and personalised approach. By sharing necessary information with experts, coordinating care effectively and addressing non-cognitive symptoms, it is possible to enhance the quality of life for individuals with dementia and their caregivers. The following outlines key actions to follow and resources available for managing dementia effectively.

Information and Support

- Provide relevant information tailored to the individual's condition and stage of dementia.
- Offer oral and written explanations about their dementia subtype, expected changes, and available healthcare professionals and support teams.
- Discuss the impact of dementia on driving, emphasising the importance of notifying the Driver and Vehicle Licensing Agency (DVLA) and car insurers.
- Share resources, such as factsheets from organisations like Dementia UK and the Alzheimer's Society, to assist in decision-making regarding driving cessation.

Legal & Advocacy: Planning Ahead

- Educate the patient and their family about their legal rights and responsibilities.

- Inform them about reasonable adjustments available under the Equality Act 2010 if they are working or seeking employment.
- Provide information on local support groups, online forums, national charities, financial and legal advice services and advocacy services.
- Encourage discussions about planning for the future, including lasting power of attorney, advance statements as well as decisions regarding care preferences, place of care and place of death.
- Emphasise that these decisions can be reviewed and modified as needed.

Care Coordination
- Ensure the patient has a designated care manager and a regularly reviewed care plan.
- Assign a single named health or social care professional responsible for coordinating their care.
- Regularly receive an assessment for dementia-related needs that may have newly emerged since the last checkup and provide additional support if required.
- Be sure to consider safeguarding concerns, carer stress and comorbidities.

Medication and Treatment
- Monitor physical and mental health and manage other long-term conditions.
- Evaluate the response to dementia treatments, adjusting dosages if necessary.

- Review medication regularly, minimising polypharmacy and avoiding drugs that impair cognition.
- Use validated tools for assessing anticholinergic burden.
- Seek specialist advice for complex cases, or if non-cognitive symptoms (e.g., behavioural and psychological symptoms of dementia) persist.

Managing Non-Cognitive Symptoms
- Prioritise a structured assessment to identify and address causes of distress.
- Offer psychosocial and environmental interventions to reduce distress.
- Provide personalised activities to promote engagement and interest.
- Consider antipsychotics for severe distress or risk of self-harm, but use them cautiously, discussing both the benefits and harms with the person and their family.
- Be sure to factor in the unique considerations when treating individuals with Lewy body dementia or Parkinson's disease dementia.

Additional Considerations
- Address depression and anxiety using psychological treatments and reserve antidepressants for severe cases.
- Develop personalised approaches to manage sleep problems, such as through some sun exposure during exercise or other activities during the day.
- Refer to specific guidelines for managing dementia in Parkinson's disease cases.

Managing End-of-Life Care in Dementia: A Compassionate Approach

End-of-life care in dementia focuses on enhancing the quality of life, preserving function and ensuring comfort for individuals with dementia. It requires a holistic approach, involving early planning, personalised care and support for both the person with dementia and their family/carer. By considering the specific needs and challenges associated with end-of-life care in dementia, healthcare professionals can strive to provide the best possible support during this difficult time. There is an entire chapter in this book that deals with the legal aspects of dementia care. Here, we briefly cover the following lists that highlight key considerations and approaches for managing end-of-life care in dementia.

Plan Ahead

Encourage early planning while the patient is in the earlier stages of dementia and involve both the patient and their family/carer in the process whenever possible. Key considerations include:

- Advance decisions: statements of future treatment wishes, including treatment refusal
- Lasting power of attorney: designating a decision-maker when the person lacks capacity
- Preferred place of care plan: recording preferences for future care, including place of death
- Making a will
- Regularly reviewing and updating these plans as needed
- Anticipatory Healthcare Planning: discussing and making plans for the course of the patient's care extending into the future (e.g., carer information, support plans, emergency

treatment, CPR decisions and other personal priorities) with their doctor, families/friends and other healthcare professionals
- Establishing that in the absence of the patient's mental capacity, decisions would be made based on decision-making principles that prioritise their best interest

Personalised Care
- Emphasise individualised care and a shared decision-making process through sufficient communication among the patient, their family/carer and the healthcare team.
- Avoid aggressive, burdensome or futile treatments.
- Ensure continuity and coordination of care across various services involved in the person's care.

Psychosocial and Spiritual Support
- Psychosocial and spiritual support must also be provided for both the patient and their family/carer to ensure that they maintain their mental wellbeing throughout their journey.
- Recognise and openly discuss the terminal stage of the disease with the family/carer in a timely manner, topics including the use of any end-of-life medications and their effects and potential side effects.
- Assess and help fulfil the needs of the family/carer through social support, educational support on palliative care aspects and bereavement support.

Dealing with Specific End-of-Life Issues

a) Eating and Drinking:
- Encourage eating and drinking as long as possible for nutritional needs.
- Involve speech and language therapists or dieticians if safety concerns arise.
- Avoid routine use of enteral feeding (e.g., tube feeding), unless indicated for potentially reversible comorbidities.

b) Distress or Changes in Behaviour:
- Assess and manage distress or behavioural changes and consider clinical or environmental causes such as pain, delirium or inappropriate care.
- Utilise pharmacological and non-pharmacological measures for pain management.

c) Constipation, Nausea and Loss of Appetite:
- Review the need for medications such as opioids, codeine or morphine if they cause constipation, nausea or loss of appetite.
- Manage constipation with dietary changes and laxatives.

d) Withholding or Withdrawing Treatment:
- Follow ethical and legal principles. As doctors, we consider the General Medical Council's standards and ethics guidance. All healthcare professionals have an obligation to make similar considerations.
- Respect the person's wishes and any advance decisions that they make regarding care and treatment, including resuscitation. Doctors may make decisions regarding this

area of care in the patient's best interest. Although it is not mandatory to involve the family in this decision, it is certainly good practice and usually facilitates a smoother management and relationship between clinicians and family members.

e) Resuscitation:
- Cardiopulmonary resuscitation is unlikely to succeed in case of cardiopulmonary arrest in severe dementia.
- Consider the person's expressed wishes and beliefs as well as the views of their family/carer and the multidisciplinary team when deciding whether to resuscitate.
- Ensure that out-of-hours services are informed about relevant decisions, such as the decision not to resuscitate and others included in their RESPECT form if completed.

CHAPTER 8:

IS THERE ANYTHING I CAN DO TO PREVENT DEMENTIA?

DR CAROL S. IGHOFOSE

LOVE YOUR BRAIN: UNDERSTANDING DEMENTIA AND THE IMPORTANCE OF BRAIN HEALTH

I hope you are now appreciating what a remarkable organ our brain is that enables us to think, learn and experience the world around us. It is the epicentre of our thoughts, emotions, memories and personality. As we age, however, the risk of developing dementia increases, posing a threat to our cognitive, behavioural, psychological and physical wellbeing. Our brain therefore deserves our attention and care in advance; understanding the impact of dementia on different regions of the brain allows us to be proactive in promoting brain health and reducing the risk of cognitive decline. There is abundant evidence to suggest that by adopting a brain-healthy lifestyle that includes physical exercise, mental stimulation, a nutritious diet, social engagement and quality sleep, we can protect our cognitive abilities, preserve our memories and lead fulfilling lives. Let's prioritise our brain health, love our brains and cherish their remarkable capacities.

PROMOTING BRAIN HEALTH AND PREVENTING DECLINE

The following information is gleaned from the *HeartMath for Brain Health* website; from Dr David Perlmutter's documentary series *Alzheimer's – The Science of Prevention* (hereinafter referred to as *A-SOP*); and from research conducted by Dr Daniel Amen, a prominent American psychiatrist.

Consider the acronyms BRIGHT MINDS for a framework on the possibility of prevention of Dementia and NEURO for strategies to improve brain health and reduce memory problems.

BRIGHT MINDS: A Comprehensive Approach to Memory Health (Adapted from Dr Daniel Amen's approach)[21]

B IS FOR BLOOD FLOW:

Maintaining good blood flow is crucial for brain health. Ageing blood vessels can pose a risk to brain cells, so it is essential to care for your blood vessels. Risk factors for blood flow problems include a history of cardiovascular diseases, including heart attacks, strokes and erectile dysfunction (which is often a precursor to other circulatory diseases) or diabetes mellitus, hypertension, traumatic brain injury, nicotine (smoking) and excessive caffeine and alcohol intake.

A lack of physical activity and exercise is often associated with many of the above risk factors and has been shown to be a causative factor for reduced blood flow to the brain. To promote healthy blood flow, engage in regular exercise for about 30 minutes a day, 5 days per week. Even if this target is not achieved immediately, starting with a lesser target is commendable. Activities that are enjoyed, shared with others, done as a group / community activity or incorporated into one's daily routine, e.g., using the stairs instead of the lifts, significantly improves the chance of being maintained and increased to the recommended target. Walking, swimming, playing tennis or dancing can be enjoyable ways to stay active.

Furthermore, information from the *A-SOP* research indicates that increased blood flow to the brain reduces inflammation and improves a growth molecule to the brain called brain-derived neurotrophic factor (BDNF) which aids in memory formation. Increased blood flow to the brain increases oxygen, improves insulin sensitivity and glucose level in the brain, aids sleep which enhances brain functions through various mechanisms and boosts mental health through the production of 'feel-good' hormones (e.g., endorphins, dopamine and serotonin levels) that decrease stress.

Some experts recommend consuming food that boosts blood flow like beets and cayenne pepper and taking supplements like ginkgo biloba. However, their effectiveness in increasing blood flow to the brain has not been sufficiently proven.

R IS FOR RETIREMENT AND AGING:

Continued learning is vital for brain health, as the saying goes: "When you stop learning, your brain starts dying." Continuously exercising your learning 'muscles' (abilities) as you advance in age is essential because ageing is the most significant risk factor for memory loss and Alzheimer's disease. To reduce this risk, make a habit of lifelong learning regardless of your age. Engage in activities that challenge your mind, pursue new hobbies that keep you entertained and focused and participate in social interactions. Avoid social isolation and loneliness as they can contribute to memory problems. Never withdraw into isolation—be intentional about joining clubs, volunteering, creating and maintaining connections or participating in group activities.

I IS FOR INFLAMMATION:

Chronic inflammation not only negatively affects your other organs but can also harm your brain. Consuming a diet high in fast food and processed foods can lead to inflammation in the body. In addition, low omega-3 levels or high C-reactive protein levels in the blood indicate increased inflammation. To combat inflammation, adopt an anti-inflammatory diet rich in whole foods (naturally grown, non-processed), increase your intake of omega-3 fatty acids through sources like fatty fish / SMASH fish (sardines, mackerel, anchovies, salmon and herring). There is some evidence that taking supplements such as probiotics and curcumin has benefits.

G IS FOR GENETICS:

Having a family history of Alzheimer's disease or other forms of dementia increases your risk. However, genetic vulnerability should be seen as a call to action rather than a predetermined outcome. Take brain health seriously if you have a family history of dementia and consider early screening for memory problems. Implement preventive measures and adhere to a brain-healthy lifestyle to reduce the impact of genetic factors. Predisposition to dementia and other chronic diseases through genetic factors is often likened to a 'loaded gun'. As scary as it may sound now, we can avoid letting it go off and change the outcome through practising preventative lifestyles.

H IS FOR HEAD TRAUMA:

Head injuries, including concussions, can be a significant risk factor for memory problems. Even injuries without a loss of consciousness can have long-term consequences. Multiple head injuries further increase the risk. Protect your brain from future injuries by wearing a helmet during activities like biking or skiing. Take precautions to avoid falls, use seat belts and practise safe behaviours such as not texting while walking or driving. Take care whilst negotiating stairs even at home. Some specialists promote hyperbaric oxygen therapy (HBOT) to aid in healing after head injuries.

T IS FOR TOXINS:

Exposure to environmental toxins has been linked to various health issues that include neurodegenerative diseases. Substances like alcohol, marijuana and other drugs can prematurely age the brain. To minimise toxin-related risks, avoid toxic exposure including air pollution, drink plenty of water to support kidney function, consume fibre-rich foods and organic produce to aid gut health, quit smoking and limit alcohol consumption to support liver health and engage in exercise and sauna sessions to promote detoxification through the skin.

Evidence from the three sources named earlier highlights the importance of our environment and the products we use on a daily basis. Be intentional about avoiding stress including from toxic relationships and unforgiveness. Make good decisions and avoid individuals with an unhealthy influence.

M IS FOR MENTAL HEALTH:

The state of your mental health significantly impacts your memory. Conditions such as depression, bipolar disorder, schizophrenia, ADD/ADHD, PTSD and chronic stress can contribute to memory problems. Adopting brain-healthy habits, including regular physical activity and a nutritious diet, is crucial. Additionally, practise cognitive techniques to overcome negative thoughts and consider seeking professional help to address mental health issues.

I IS FOR IMMUNE SYSTEM PROBLEMS AND INFECTIONS:

When the immune system is compromised, vulnerability to autoimmune disorders and infections increases, potentially impacting brain function. It is essential to take precaution against infections such as syphilis and HIV. Boost your immune system by ensuring adequate vitamin D intake and incorporating immune-boosting foods like onions, mushrooms and garlic into your diet.

If you suspect a lingering infection with lethargy, fever on and off and general fatigue, consult with your GP for proper diagnosis and treatment.

N IS FOR NEUROHORMONE ISSUES:

The brain and hormones influence each other significantly. Imbalance in hormone levels, such as thyroid, testosterone or oestrogen, can increase the risk of Alzheimer's disease and other illnesses. Consult your GP for an assessment and relevant investigations as well as optimisation of hormone levels if necessary.

D IS FOR DIABESITY:

Diabesity, a coined term that combines diabetes and obesity, has detrimental effects on brain size and function. It damages blood vessels, leading to conditions such as Alzheimer's disease, vascular dementia, strokes and hypertension. To mitigate these risks, adopt brain-healthy and balanced diet rich in fruit, vegetables, whole grains, lean proteins and omega-3 fatty acids to support brain health. Limiting the consumption of processed foods, saturated fats and sugary snacks is essential.

A-SOP highlights the importance of paying attention to conditions such as pre-diabetes. It is important to adhere to the recommended management plan by your GP, diabetes specialists and/or diabetes prevention programs available to you if this condition is identified. It is worth noting that AD is often referred to as Type 3 diabetes because of its similarities to Type 2 diabetes regarding the risk factors and the effects on the brain. It is crucial to reduce excessive alcohol intake, salt and highly processed foods. Choose food with a low glycaemic index and load, such as plant fat and fibres, nuts, seeds, herbs and spices (to enhance food taste without using salt and sugar) and SMASH fish—essentially a mediterranean-style diet. These types of food have been shown to reduce inflammation in the body including the gut. Studies also highlight the benefits of a healthy gut microbiome (improving and not destroying the 'good bacteria' and other microorganisms in our gut). Artificial sweeteners, often used to replace sugar, have been found to have adverse effects on our gut microbiome. Many individuals have benefited significantly from Time Restricted Eating (TRE) or Intermittent Fasting (IF) to avoid diabetes and obesity. Discuss this option with your GP, practice nurse or other appropriate health care professional before embarking on TRE or IF.

S IS FOR SLEEP:

Prioritising restful sleep also supports brain health. Sleep problems, including insomnia and sleep apnoea, have been linked to a higher risk of memory problems and dementia. Aim for 7-9 hours of quality sleep each night and establish a relaxing bedtime routine by waking up and going to bed at the same time daily. It is important to avoid stimulants such as caffeine and exercise near bedtime. A general rule of thumb is to have your last caffeine drink by 2:00 pm and exercise or consume alcohol no later than 3-4 hours before bedtime. If you snore or suspect sleep apnoea, seek assessment from your GP and get appropriate referral and treatment as necessary.

A-SOP research underscores the importance of the role of sleep in our circadian rhythm and glymphatic system. When we ignore our circadian rhythms and neglect to get the sleep that our bodies need, all of these natural physical processes—including the regulation of hormones (like leptin and ghrelin that control our appetite and weight loss), insulin and cortisol—are thrown into disarray. The glymphatic system is the brain's way of 'cleaning house' and getting rid of the metabolic waste products that accumulate while we are awake. Poor sleep pattern or insufficient sleep reduces the effectiveness of the glymphatic system and results in metabolic waste matter and toxins remaining instead of being properly flushed away from the brain and central nervous system, which then increases the risk of cognitive impairment and dementia, especially AD.[23]

According to Dr David Perlmutter, sleep helps reduce the risk of developing AD by "supporting healthy metabolism, lowering inflammation, improving your ability to fight off infections, supporting your microbiome and even getting help in coping with stress and increasing creativity," all of which combine to "help our brain to process information, learn new things, store information, store memories, and wash itself from the waste buildup from the previous day's activities."[23]

Dr Michael J. Breus, PhD DABSM, speaking as a guest expert for *A-SOP*, provided some good sleep hacks, gleaned from clinical research:[23]

- Have consistent sleep and wake-up times, even on the weekends
- Stop caffeine by about 2:00 pm; half of the caffeine consumed remains in your body six to eight hours after it is consumed and may take up to 10 hours to clear.
- Avoid excessive alcohol intake and do not consume alcohol for at least 3 hours before bedtime. (Nb: Bethel advocates a 'no alcohol' consumption policy).

- Stop exercise about 4 hours before bed; it raises core body temperature and generally increases alertness - both disruptive for sleep
- Avoid blue light devices, including from computer screens, tablets, cell phones, and even television. When blue light hits melanopsin cells in our eyes, it turns off the melatonin faucet. Melatonin is needed for sleep. So blue light exposure at night will stimulate wakefulness and prevent melatonin production which is necessary for sleep.
- Get sunlight every morning -sunlight, which is mostly blue light in the mornings, equally turns off melatonin production. Ideally within 30 mins of waking up - walk to the window, open the curtains and say "good morning" to the sunlight. Your brain will know it's daytime and time to wake up. Needless to say, being out in the fresh air and careful exposure to the various spectrums of sunlight is generally beneficial, including to guide our bodies in their sleep and wakeful states.

There is also enough evidence to support practising prayer and meditation to aid sleep and reduce stress; Supplements including Vit D, melatonin may be taken but should always be guided by your GP or hospital consultants/specialists. This may require having a blood test to check the exact level of Vitamin D or vit B & folate levels, e.g., to guide replacement.

NEURO: A Framework for Implementing Preventative Strategies for Dementia (Adapted from the authors of *Preventing Alzheimer's: Our Most Urgent Health Care Priority*)[22]

The acronym NEURO was coined to help us all remember the most important lifestyle elements in the treatment and prevention of Alzheimer's disease based on the evidence that ageing does not necessarily have to lead to cognitive decline. Both BRIGHT MINDS and NEURO are convenient toolkits that encourage and empower you to remember to love and protect your brain, in the quest to reduce the chances of developing dementia.

N FOR NUTRITION:

Refer back to 'Diabesity' above. The following are key empowering steps from the research referenced:

1. Reduce processed sugars
2. Reduce saturated fat (We advise increase monounsaturated and polyunsaturated fats such as olive oil, avocados, SMASH fish
3. Reduce animal products (meat, dairy, cheese)
4. Reduce processed foods
5. Consume more plants of all varieties, especially greens and beans
6. Increase fruit consumption, especially berries
7. Reduce salt consumption

E FOR EXERCISE:

Exercise and physical activities have a direct positive impact on every system in our bodies. Dr Daivid Perlmutter says: "If a drug were to be developed that mimicked the effects of exercise, it would absolutely be a blockbuster drug. Physicians would be prescribing it to the young, to the old, to the sick and to the healthy. And yet all of us have the ability to take advantage of exercise every single day."[23] Despite this knowledge about exercise and physical activities, however, many of us do not take advantage of the benefits of keeping our bodies moving regularly and sufficiently, ideally starting from very early in life.

The most beneficial types of activities that promote brain health and potentially help reverse cognitive impairment include the following:

1. A regimented exercise program involving extensive aerobic exercise on a regular basis
2. Leg strengthening exercises to increase blood flow to the heart and the brain
3. Regular movement throughout the day

U FOR UNWIND (STRESS MANAGEMENT):

Research findings to date emphasise several effective practices that help manage stress:

1. Identify your good and bad stress.
2. Work towards increasing good (meaning purpose-driven and success-oriented) stress and reduce bad stress.
3. Practise meditation and mindfulness techniques throughout the day.

R FOR RESTORATIVE SLEEP:

Important information about sleep has been discussed under 'Sleep' above; please refer to the below to refresh your mind. What we know to date about sleep and its effect on the brain includes the following:

1. Restorative sleep includes quality and quantity of sleep. This spans around 7 to 9 hours, involves going into deep sleep through the different phases of sleep on repeat several times per night.
2. This process facilitates memory and cognitive consolidation and organisation as well as detoxification.
3. Almost everyone can achieve ultimate restorative sleep over time through consistent sleep hygiene implementation as well as cognitive behavioural techniques.
4. If one suspects the possibility of sleep apnoea, they should immediately get tested for it because untreated sleep apnoea and other sleep disorders can significantly increase one's risk for dementia, particularly Alzheimer's disease.

O FOR OPTIMISE:

Cognitive optimising appears to be most effectively achieved in the following cases:

1. When individuals carry out complex tasks that involve multiple cognitive domains of the brain, such as learning musical instruments or languages and leading projects (job complexity has a greater effect on building cognitive reserve)
2. When activities are challenging, thus continually pushing the brain to adapt
3. When activities are purpose-driven, creating positive stress for the brain

These science-backed strategies can help you circumvent risk factors associated with memory loss, promote brain health and ultimately reduce dementia risk. Remember: most of these risk factors are preventable or treatable, and you can enhance your cognitive wellbeing. Above all, love your brain—be intentional about caring for it.

REFERENCES FOR CHAPTERS 7 &8

1. Risk factors for dementia. BMJ Best Practice. https://bestpractice.bmj.com/topics/en-gb/491
2. Barrett A. Mild cognitive impairment: An update. *Irish Medical Journal.* 2014;107(2):42-45.
3. Diagnosis and management of dementia: A guide for primary care. Royal College of General Practitioners. Published 2013. https://www.rcgp.org.uk/clinical-and-research/resources/toolkits/dementia-toolkit.aspx
4. Loy CT, Schofield PR, Turner AM, Kwok JB. Genetics of dementia. *The Lancet.* 2014;383(9919):828-840. doi:https://doi.org/10.1016/S0140-6736(13)60630-3
5. Schott JM. Neurodegenerative diseases. *Medicine.* 2020;48(5):307-314.
6. Winblad B, Amouyel P, Andrieu S, et al. Defeating Alzheimer's disease and other dementias: a priority for European science and society. *The Lancet Neurology.* 2016;15(5):455-532. doi:https://doi.org/10.1016/S1474-4422(16)00062-4
7. Savva GM. Incidence of dementia in a representative cohort of elderly and the effect of stroke: The Rotterdam Study. *Neurology.* 2010;70(16):1322-1328.
8. Livingston G, Huntley J, Sommerlad A, et al. Dementia prevention, intervention, and care: 2020 report of the Lancet Commission. *The Lancet.* 2020;396(10248):413-446.
9. Dementia: Applying All Our Health. Public Health England. Published 2016. Accessed 2023. https://www.gov.uk/government/publications/dementia-applying-all-our-health/dementia-applying-all-our-health

10. Ridley NJ, Draper B, Withall A. Alcohol-related dementia: an update of the evidence. *Alzheimer's Research & Therapy.* 2013;5(1):3. doi:https://doi.org/10.1186/alzrt157
11. Risk reduction of cognitive decline and dementia: WHO guidelines. World Health Organization. Published 2019. https://apps.who.int/iris/handle/10665/312180
12. Dementia: Assessment, management and support for people living with dementia and their carers. London: National Institute for Health and Care Excellence (NICE). Published June 2018.
13. Dementia: a public health priority. World Health Organization. Published 2012. https://apps.who.int/iris/handle/10665/75263
14. Systemic sclerosis (scleroderma) - Symptoms, diagnosis and treatment. BMJ Best Practice. Published 2020. Accessed 2023. https://bestpractice.bmj.com/topics/en-gb/295
15. Barrett AM, Eslinger PJ. The Psychological and Emotional Consequences of Stroke. *Physical Medicine and Rehabilitation Clinics of North America.* 2014;25(3):697-715.
16. Kales HC, Gitlin LN, Lyketsos CG. Assessment and management of behavioral and psychological symptoms of dementia. *BMJ.* 2015;350:h369. Published 2015. doi:10.1136/bmj.h369
17. Robinson L, Tang E, Taylor JP. Dementia: timely diagnosis and early intervention. *BMJ.* 2015;350:h3029. Published 2015. doi:10.1136/bmj.h3029
18. Dementia Profile. Public Health England. Published 2019. Accessed 2023. https://fingertips.phe.org.uk/profile-group/mental-health/profile/dementia

19. Prince M, Knapp M, Guerchet M, et al. Dementia UK: Update. Alzheimer's Society. Published 2014. http://www.alzheimers.org.uk/dementiauk
20. Kane M, Terry G. Dementia 2015: Aiming higher to transform lives. Alzheimer's Society. Published 2015. http://www.alzheimers.org.uk/dementia2015
21. BRIGHT MINDS—Proven Ways to Reduce the Risk of Alzheimer's Disease and Dementia. Amen Clinics. Published 2022. Accessed 2023. https://www.amenclinics.com/blog/bright-minds-proven-ways-to-reduce-the-risk-of-alzheimers-disease-and-dementia/
22. Sherzai D, Sherzai A. Preventing Alzheimer's: Our Most Urgent Health Care Priority. *American Journal of Lifestyle Medicine*. 2019;13(5):451-461. doi:https://doi.org/10.1177/1559827619843465
23. Perlmutter D. Alzheimer's – The Science of Prevention. Published online 2020. https://scienceofprevention.com/

CHAPTER 9:

COMMON QUESTIONS AND ANSWERS AND UNIQUE DEMENTIA QUOTES

MRS ELAINE RICHARDS

Being in a position where a family member or friend has or is in the process of being examined or diagnosed with dementia can be an overwhelming experience.

Some people tackle this position head-on, wanting to know everything there is to know about the process and the condition; others 'stick their head in the sand' because they can't cope with imagining their loved one having the condition or themselves having to deal with it. And many fall somewhere in the middle—possibly torn between conflicted feelings. But whichever side you're on, this book is here to help.

I hope that this chapter will help you navigate through some of the common questions or misconceptions about dementia that individuals with dementia and their family and friends may have. In conjunction with the other chapters of the book, this chapter will help put the pieces of information together and fill the gaps in between so that we are more prepared for and more knowledgeable about what dementia entails.

1. **"It's a waste of time—it's too difficult and takes too long to get a diagnosis."**

    In truth, the process to get diagnosed with dementia can indeed be a long one. To begin with, even before the actual process of diagnosis, there can be many factors that contribute to the delay: from the patient's reluctance to meet with a GP to their denial about what their symptoms may indicate. Then, when they have gotten through all these hurdles, the process of diagnosis itself begins, which can take a long time; however, it will provide a sense of relief to know that your loved one is finally in good hands and is getting the most appropriate help in place. Early interaction with relevant services is a good idea, so that you can increase the amount of help you are getting from their services as needed over time.

2. **Don't be embarrassed to ask for help!**
   Many of us mistakenly believe that we should be able to cope with anything that life throws at us. We think that we can manage, but there will be times when we must be realistic and honest with ourselves about what is happening at home. Our loved ones with dementia may become less physically and mentally capable due to diminishing brain function or awareness, and having a person they don't remember undertaking personal care may be distressing for them. Asking for help from carers trained to work in this field may help alleviate such tension; for instance, they can intervene in a situation where a family member is trying to force a care activity which their loved one with dementia does not want to do.

3. **"What is the difference between dementia and Alzheimer's?"**
   Dementia is what we could call an umbrella term—a term that encompasses different types of the condition. There are several types of Dementia, one of which is Alzheimer's disease (over 50% of cases); other types include vascular dementia, Lewy body dementia and frontotemporal dementia.

   Different types of dementia have different presentations, but they also overlap; the effects of dementia can be different on different individuals, so it is hard to predict the exact symptoms a person will experience. What helps or doesn't help will also depend on the patient. It is, therefore, important for your loved one to have the correct diagnosis so that the best course of treatment and care can be tailor-made for them.

It is up to us as carers and family to learn as much as we can about the changes in our loved one with dementia so that their life can be as enjoyable as we would like ours to be. The smile that brightens up their face when we, after some trial and error, find something that they enjoy (e.g., singing, playing music or taking a walk in the park) will be rewarding beyond all measure.

4. **"Don't panic Mr Mannering" / "Keep Calm and Carry On!"**
These quotes are so much easier said than done when it comes to caring for someone with dementia.

You may have started noticing that your loved one is not as engaging, as mindful or as physically able as they used to be, and it has dawned on you just now that they may possibly have dementia. Or you may already be in the thick of it, caring for a family member in an advanced stage of dementia. Wherever you are on your journey, always remember to save yourself from responsibility overload. This book contains information about many avenues of support that you can tap into, so be sure to check them out. Being stressed causes our own health to fail; if we are now on a journey to become carers, we need to prioritise being in good health ourselves in order to care for our loved ones.

In addition, there will be times when others make light of the impact that dementia can have on a family; the false belief that one simply has to 'get on with it' downplays the seriousness of challenges that families face during the care of their loved ones living with dementia. As 3 John 1:2 says, "Beloved, I wish above all things that thou mayest prosper and be in health, even as thy soul prospereth." As Christians we must hold our peace despite what others say.

5. **"S/he won't listen" / "S/he is doing this to wind me up"**
During the progression of dementia, there are times when the affected person is lucid, meaning they are aware of time and space and able to think clearly and rationally; and other times when they are not able to process where they are, what time/year it is or who they are living with.

Imagine yourself, their carer, being frustrated that they 'don't want to listen or do as they are asked'—then imagine the absolute fear that the person with dementia would experience in the same situation where they have no clue who you are, where they are and what you're asking them to do.

When this happens in real life, try not to correct them too harshly or yell at them but rather to guide them by gently repeating what you are asking them to do. When you ask, they may immediately forget what you asked, so be prepared to ask in short sentences and repeat when necessary. In addition, if you are in situations where they do things that frustrate you, keep your calm and try putting yourself in their position first. For example, if they put away valuables like house keys and forget where they placed them, do not criticise them for having done so because it was *not* their intention to lose the keys. It'd be more beneficial for you to put away your valuables in advance for future safety purposes so that they are not within the patient's reach next time.

The diagnosis of dementia comes because the person has memory impairment, so forgiveness of their behaviours *and* of your frustrations is key.

Just remember the Fruit of the Spirit: love, joy, peace, longsuffering, gentleness, goodness, faith, meekness and temperance (Galatians 5:22-23). Every single one of those elements needs to be in action when looking after someone with dementia. And if you're struggling, it may be better to have help to look after your loved one so that you don't end up resenting them; that way, you can observe and support them rather than try to do it all on your own.

It's not that they won't listen or that they are trying to wind you up; it's just that they simply don't understand what you're asking them to do. Patience is a virtue, so we have to try our very best to exercise it.

6. **"We don't put our families in homes"**
There are certain cultural traditions or beliefs which have been handed down through the generations, one of which is that the sick or elderly should be looked after at home

by family members, not placed into care homes. Doing so, of course, is manageable in many cases, but there are some situations where, due to various factors, it may pose serious challenges and even safety concerns.

In the past, many families lived in close-knit communities, where they had relatives and friends living in close proximity who could help take care of those who were not well, which then became a shared responsibility. Over time, however, many families moved to live farther away from one another and from the churches they attend, and therefore the number of available carers has depleted.

The most appropriate care for a patient may be in their own home (with or without assistance), in another family member's home, a hospital, an assisted living facility, a care home or a nursing home—there is no right or wrong in this case. You should feel absolutely no shame in your loved one being cared for outside your home. Even though the patient is cared for elsewhere, family members should still be respected and supported for having to discuss and make difficult decisions concerning the care of their loved one.

Thank God we live in a world where we can access health and social care with trained workers who can offer their help to those in need.

7. **"How do I tell them that their brother/sister has died?"**
Depending on the degree of memory loss, the carers/family of the person with dementia have to agree whether or not to inform the patient of a bereavement. The individual with

dementia may be living in the past as long-term memory is often the last to be forgotten. It may be wise not to tell the person if it would be too upsetting for them, so this delicate decision has to be made with care and in the best interest of the patient. It would upset the patient, for instance, if we were to tell them that their sibling or loved one has passed away in their non-lucid state; the individual may live in old memories from decades ago and believe that they are still alive when someone breaks this news to them, which may cause an intense reaction of confusion, distress and anxiety. If the individual speaks as if we were still living in the past, it would be kinder to indulge them than to bluntly correct them.

If you need professional help on this matter, do feel free to speak with your GP or an advisor from one of the care organisations.

8. **"You must bring them to church!"**
How many times have we heard this one? Hopefully, having read the explanations of many difficulties that come with the condition, we will all be more tolerant and understanding of the vulnerabilities of people living with dementia.

As much as we want to keep our loved ones in the routines that they are familiar and comfortable with, there may come a time when, even while singing their favourite songs and tapping to the beat, they may exhibit behaviour that is not appropriate for the church or other public settings and require us to step in as their carers. We should be fiercely protective of our loved ones whoever they are and whatever their age or illness—it may sometimes be better for them in some cases to stay home or in their safe environment than perhaps to be exposed to potential danger . We have to be mindful of the safeguarding aspects of their care and steer clear of situations where they would be placed in vulnerable positions.

Fortunately, most churches nowadays use Zoom or other streaming platforms, where the person with dementia can still join the service and sing to their heart's content during and till after the service. Many, if not all, churches also have a hospitality team to make house calls on the sick/homebound or visit them at healthcare facilities; and a pastoral team to offer Lord's Supper/Communion. The patient's spiritual care is as important as their physical care!

There is no reason for the person with dementia to miss out on anything. You may take the person out of the church but can't take the church out of the person! There are many ways to facilitate their enjoyable pastimes, and part of our care is to find those ways and be creative if necessary.

9. **"I can't get them in the car"**

We are fortunate in the UK to have a number of free and low-fee transportation facilities available to the elderly and to those with illnesses. If you contact your local Dementia UK facility, Social Services, GP Surgery, Volunteering Agency, Age UK, Ring & Ride, Dial-a-Ride or other organisations, you will find an appropriate local mode of transportation with or without assistance provided, which you can access to accompany your loved one to their appointments. Some of these agencies also provide transportation to specific lunch clubs, so that the person with dementia (and their carer) would be able to enjoy trips out for a social get-together if they wish and if appropriate.

10. "Where do we go to learn more about dementia?"

Dementia UK, Alzheimer's Society and the NHS are just three of the many excellent sources of information available that you can use to learn about dementia. Each organisation has a range of resources, clinicians and support workers to help patients diagnosed with dementia and their families. Alzheimer's Society, for instance, has online courses available that provide insight into different aspects of dementia and also runs support groups in many areas (visit their website for more information).

When we are diagnosed with a health condition such as diabetes, hypertension or asthma, we often try to find out as much as we can about the condition so that we will be best informed about our health. The same goes for when we have a family member diagnosed with dementia; we should gather as much credible information as possible about dementia because, due to the very nature of the condition, it is likely that the patient cannot do their own research and over time will not remember that information. We have to become their advocates, just as Jesus became our Advocate and stepped in on our behalf to represent us in our best interest.

11. Is dementia a mental illness?

No. Dementia is categorised as a Neurocognitive Disorder (NCD) in the Diagnostic and Statistical Manual of Mental Disorders (DSM-5) as well as in the International Classification of Diseases (ICD-10), both of which are published by the World Health Organization.

Individuals demonstrating features of psychiatric or behavioural disturbances of dementia may display signs and symptoms of mental illness, e.g., low mood, excessive lethargy, lack of motivation, agitation, hallucination and delusions. However, although there may be an overlap, these symptoms alone do not meet the criteria for a diagnosis of dementia. The key differentiator of a neurocognitive disorder versus a mental illness is the gradual and significant cognitive decline. Neurocognitive disorders result from structural or functional changes in the brain, which are often associated with underlying neurodegenerative processes, vascular issues or other brain-related conditions, whereas mental illnesses are defined by emotional and behavioural disturbances.

DEMENTIA QUOTES FOR INSPIRATION AND EMPOWERMENT

"Although your loved one may not remember you or might do things that frustrate you, this is the time when he needs you the most."
Angie Nunez Merryman

"Those with dementia are still people, and they still have stories, and they still have character, and they are all individuals, and they are all unique. And they just need to be interacted with on a human level." *Carey Mulligan*

"Kindness can transform someone's dark moment with a blaze of light. You'll never know how much your caring matters. Make a difference for another day." *Amy Leigh Mercree*

"Too often we underestimate the power of a touch, a smile, a kind word, a listening ear, an honest compliment, or the smallest act of caring, all of which have the potential to turn a life around." *Leo Buscaglia*

"Sometimes you will never know the value of a moment until it becomes a memory." *Dr Seuss*

"Don't dwell on the disease. Value the moments, the pearls of wisdom, their smile and humour." *Linda Brendle*

"Casting all your care upon him; for he careth for you." *1 Peter 5:7 (KJV)*

"Let us run with patience the race that is set before us." *Hebrews 12:1b (KJV)*

CHAPTER 10:

CONCLUSION

DR CAROL S. IGHOFOSE

Dementia is a complex and challenging condition that affects millions of individuals worldwide. It gradually robs people of their cognitive abilities and compromises their independence and quality of life. However, by understanding the nature of the condition and implementing appropriate and effective strategies, we can provide compassionate care for individuals living with dementia, including those we refer to in Bethel as our 'Treasured Saints', and support their loved ones who carry the weight of responsibility on their shoulders as carers.

In this book we have explored the key aspects of dementia including its causes, risk factors, signs and symptoms, diagnosis and management. We have learned that early detection and diagnosis are crucial for optimising treatment and support options. Fostering a supportive environment, promoting cognitive stimulation and engaging in meaningful activities can all combine to greatly enhance the wellbeing of individuals with dementia.

Furthermore, we have discussed the importance of intensive personalised care, prioritising the individual's needs and preferences and focusing on maintaining their dignity and autonomy. By adopting a multidisciplinary approach, involving healthcare professionals, caregivers and support networks, we can ensure a comprehensive and holistic care experience for dementia patients.

End-of-life care in dementia requires special attention and sensitivity. We have explored the principles of palliative care which emphasise improving the quality of life, maximising comfort and respecting the person's wishes and preferences. By engaging in early planning, involving the person and their family/carer and providing psychosocial and spiritual support, we can ease the journey towards the end of life for individuals with dementia and their loved ones.

While dementia presents significant challenges, we must approach it with empathy, compassion and commitment. By better informing ourselves through research and education and implementing individualised strategies, we can make a positive difference in the lives of those living with dementia, offering them comfort, positivity and support throughout their journey.

1 Thessalonians 5:23 reminds us, "And the very God of peace sanctify you wholly; and I pray God your whole spirit and soul and body be preserved blameless unto the coming of our Lord Jesus Christ." The sanctification in this verse refers to the continuation of the sanctification that is begun at the beginning of the Christian life. The word "wholly" indicates that it is a perfected or completed state of sanctification that Paul desired the Thessalonians to possess, encompassing their spirit, soul and body. Our spirit represents the ruling faculty that connects us with God, the soul embodies our mind, will and emotions and our body links us to the material world. Paul yearned for their entirety to be presented perfect and intact on the day of the Lord's coming.

In essence, while dementia may affect our bodies and souls to some extent, our spirits remain intact—out of the reach of dementia.

Teepa Snow, a renowned dementia specialist once said, "Dementia does not rob someone of their dignity; it's our reaction to them that does." She further adds, "Our brains may be different, but if we link our hands together, there is nothing that we cannot overcome." In the journey of facing the unknown and the inevitable, we draw strength from one another. With love as our cornerstone and compassion as our guide, we join our hands and hearts in solidarity to maximise all our collective abilities and strengths as we open our arms wide to embrace individuals with dementia and their carers and ensure that they do not feel alone in their fight against the disease. We commit to this cause, driven by our shared love for God and faith in His words.

The road ahead seems overwhelming, but we must strive on, taking solace in the guiding words of the Lord to Zerubbabel: "Not by might nor by power, but by my Spirit" (Zechariah 4:6). In this powerful affirmation, we find the courage to forge ahead, knowing that our efforts are bolstered not merely by our own strength, but by the overarching force of the divine and sovereign, the El Bethel, that unites us all.

Let us walk hand in hand, uplifting each other with unwavering love, care and understanding.

GLOSSARY OF TERMS

Dementia: An umbrella term used to describe a group of conditions that affect the brain and cause problems with memory, thinking and daily functioning. People with dementia may have difficulty remembering things, making decisions, communicating and performing everyday tasks. The condition is often progressive, meaning that it worsens over time. Common types of dementia include Alzheimer's disease, vascular dementia and Lewy body dementia. Dementia can have a significant impact on a person's life and the lives of their loved ones, but with understanding, support and appropriate care, individuals with dementia can continue to live fulfilling lives.

Early-onset (or young-onset) dementia: Generally defined as dementia that develops before the age of 65 years.

Mild cognitive impairment (MCI): Cognitive impairment that does not fulfil the diagnostic criteria for dementia; for example, only one cognitive domain is affected, or the deficits do not significantly affect daily activities. MCI is often clinically considered a pre-dementia state, but not always.

Brain-Derived Neurotrophic Factor (BDNF): A protein that plays a crucial role in promoting the growth, survival and function of neurons in the brain. It is involved in synaptic plasticity and is essential for learning, memory and overall cognitive function.

Exercise: Refers to physical activity that is planned, structured, repetitive and aimed at improving or maintaining physical fitness and overall health. It involves various activities such as cardiovascular exercises, strength training, flexibility exercises and balance exercises.

Physical Activity: Any bodily movement produced by skeletal muscles that results in energy expenditure. It includes both planned exercise activities and everyday activities like walking, gardening and housework.

Inflammation: A natural response of the body's immune system to injury, infection or harmful stimuli. It involves the release of immune cells, cytokines and other molecules to protect the body and initiate the healing process. However, chronic inflammation is an abnormal response to various insults to our bodies, including prolonged stress and unhealthy food, which contributes to various health issues ultimately resulting in chronic illnesses such as dementia.

Microbiome: The collection of microbes as well as their genetic material and the metabolic products that they manufacture from the bacteria that naturally live within our bodies. Their metabolism helps determine how we process our food and influences our hormones and our neurotransmitters.

Gut Microbiome: Refers to the community of trillions of microorganisms, including bacteria, viruses, fungi and other microbes, that reside in the gastrointestinal tract (gut). It plays a crucial role in digestion, metabolism, immune function and overall health.

Prebiotics: Non-digestible dietary fibres that promote the growth and activity of beneficial gut bacteria. They serve as food for probiotics (good bacteria) and support a healthy gut microbiome.

Probiotics: Live beneficial microorganisms, primarily bacteria and sometimes yeasts, that confer health benefits on the individual (the host) when consumed in adequate amounts. They promote a balanced gut microbiome and support digestive health and overall wellbeing.

Intermittent Fasting: An eating pattern that cycles between periods of eating and fasting. It does not prescribe specific food choices but focuses on the timing of meals to promote various health benefits, such as improved metabolism, insulin sensitivity and weight management.

Time-Restricted Eating: A form of intermittent fasting that restricts the eating window to a specific time frame each day. It involves consuming all daily caloric intake within a set period, typically 8-12 hours, and fasting for the remaining hours.

Mediterranean-Style Diet: A dietary pattern inspired by the traditional eating habits of countries bordering the Mediterranean. It emphasises consumption of fruit, vegetables, whole grains, legumes, nuts, seeds, olive oil and fish as well as a moderate amount of poultry and dairy. Red meat and processed foods are limited.

Saturated Fats: A type of dietary fat predominantly found in animal products like meat, butter and dairy as well as some plant oils like coconut oil and palm oil. Consuming excessive amounts of saturated fats has been linked to increased risk of heart disease and other health issues. It should be noted that there is an ongoing debate about the health benefits of coconut oil due to its saturated fat content; however, coconut also contains MCTs that are considered a healthy energy source and can be beneficial when consumed in moderation.

Unsaturated Fats: A type of dietary fat found in plant-based oils, nuts, seeds, avocados and fatty fish. Unlike saturated fats, they are considered heart-healthy and can help improve cholesterol levels and reduce the risk of heart disease. Unsaturated fats are further divided into monounsaturated and polyunsaturated fats.

LPA: A lasting power of attorney (LPA) is a legal document that lets you (the 'donor') appoint one or more people (known as 'attorneys') to help you make decisions or to make decisions on your behalf.

Source: https://www.gov.uk/power-of-attorney

Will: A legal document in which a person (the testator) declares their intention as to what should happen to their estate after their death, and which is executed in accordance with certain legal formalities.

Source: https://uk.practicallaw.thomsonreuters.com/4-382-6317?transitionType=Default&contextData=(sc.Default)&firstPage=true

Deputy: A deputy is a person the Court of Protection appoints to make decisions for you. They can do this when you've lost capacity to make decisions yourself. A deputy is different to an attorney. An attorney is someone you appoint yourself, while you still have capacity (see LPA above)."

source: https://www.mind.org.uk/information-support/legal-rights/mental-capacity-act-2005/deputies/#WhatIsADeputy

John's Campaign: The right of relatives or carers to stay with people with dementia in hospitals outside of visiting times, which applies to all hospital settings and some care homes. As a carer you can make enquiries from the hospital to which your relative is admitted.

To get in touch, please email Julia Jones (julia-jones@talk21.com) or Nicci Gerrard (nicci.gerrard@icloud.com). Julia can also be reached by phone at 01245 231898.

You may follow John's Campaign on Facebook and on https://johnscampaign.org.uk.

ACKNOWLEDGMENTS

⯐

MRS ELAINE RICHARDS

We must thank everyone in our lives for their love and support, starting with our wonderful parents—we wouldn't be here without them! We express our sincerest gratitude to them for having nurtured us to develop strong minds that withstand any weather and to always reach out to others in need. Their teaching has led to our project in which we share with a broader audience our experience, knowledge and expertise in dementia care whose aspects have baffled and frustrated so many around the world.

To Dr Carol Ighofose for her vision to bring together this incredible team of co-authors to write this book. We truly value each member of our team—getting to know one another during our roadshows in spreading dementia awareness has been a blessing.

To our editor, Rosamund Leigh, who clearly thrives on little sleep! Her meticulous attention to detail and gentle suggestions helped us improve our articulation of thoughts.

We must, of course, thank Dementia UK for their support and endorsement. They connected us with Elene Scantlebury, Dementia UK Ambassador, who kindly provided us with a detailed account of the ups and downs of her personal experience as a carer for her mother.

To Jacqueline Nicely, our friend and sister, for being so gracious by sharing her firsthand experience with her husband Hugh—thank you.

To all our families and friends for their help and guidance, either by reading our chapters or by giving us a nudge in the right direction to cultivate our thoughts. They helped to remind us of the real-life issues of living with those with dementia.

We acknowledge and thank our Presiding Bishop Dexter Edmund, the Bethel UK Board of Bishops, our Pastors and Leaders, who have supported us in our endeavours.

In memory of our dearly departed Bishop Sydney Alexander Dunn, Bishop Herman D Brown, Bishop Arnold G Miller, Bishop Gerald E Edmund, Bishop Martin H Simmonds and their wives, who founded our Church, Bethel Apostolic Church of Jesus Christ UK, where we continue to worship and have fellowship with one another.

To the 'Treasured Saints' of Bethel, who have unselfishly given their time and effort to support the Church over many decades. The proceeds of this book will go towards their department to enable practical improvements in the care and service that we offer as a church community.

We thank Rianna Simmonds for using her graphic design skills to produce a wonderful pictorial cover that perfectly matches the topic of the book.

Credit goes to Isio Ighofose for his witty pictorial representation of the hand-brain analogy.

Our deepest gratitude to all the carers and other professionals for their work in dementia care. Whether you are a paid carer who works for the NHS, social services, legal teams, or any private organisations, or are an unpaid carer caring for your loved ones, we thank you for your commitment and pray that your endeavours reach thousands more.

Last but certainly not least, we acknowledge and thank our Lord and Saviour Jesus Christ for giving us a mind to work together to share Dr Carol's vision in the production and publication of this book. Had God not inspired her, had He not shown a way to bring the writers and contributors together, we would not be in this place of gratitude that we now find ourselves in.

All glory be to God for His everlasting love towards us. It is in His power that we share our inspirations, anecdotes and knowledge with you, the reader. We sincerely pray that having read through the pages of this book, you find yourself more informed, equipped, enlightened, motivated and empowered to make steps to improve the care of your loved ones, but also that you feel inspired to extend your support to others in need.

Finally, we pay special tribute to the mother of one of the authors, Elene Maynard-Scantlebury. Known as 'Sis' or 'Lil Sis' Maynard, she lived with dementia in her later years, and sadly left us just before the publication of this book. May she rest in eternal peace.

ABOUT THE AUTHORS

REV. DR JOYPHEN HENRY

Rev. Dr Joyphen Henry is a theologian and experienced Bible teacher. She is a woman of faith who believes in the unfailing power of prayer. She was always aware of God's calling on her life as an evangelist from an early age. It was no surprise when she made several missionary trips to Hungary, ministering the gospel in cities across the country.

Dr Joy earned two master's degrees in leadership, and theology and then later completed a PhD program with her PhD thesis exploring how Pentecostal theology addresses dementia. She is keen to raise awareness of God's unfailing love for people living with dementia and to dispel negative theological perceptions associated with the disease. She notably established a women's pastors forum with the goal of better equipping women pastors. She also co-founded a support group for pastors' wives, which provided women with a safe space to share their experiences and learn from one another. She has extensive experience in church planting and public speech at conferences. She is a mentor and counsellor with profound interests in leadership and management in both the church and secular domains.

Apart from her work in the church, Dr Joy is a motivator and inspirational woman who seeks to help people achieve their full potential and be grateful to God for even the smallest blessings. She serves as chairperson for an NHS Trust Associate Hospital Managers Panel. She is a retired Fellow of the Chartered Association of Certified Accountants (FCCA) and has held several senior positions including group accountant and director. She has also developed and delivered finance training for directors as well as finance and business training for women in the UK.

In her spare time, Dr Joy enjoys reading, walking, horse riding and visiting botanical gardens. She loves spending time with her two grandchildren who bring her immense joy.

JACQUELINE NICELY

The daughter of Leonard & Sylvia Clarke who emigrated from the beautiful island of St. Kitts in the early 1960s, Jacqueline Nicely was born, raised and educated in Birmingham.

Jacqueline worked in the automotive and logistics industries before moving into the public sector. She has worked in the emergency services for the last 30 years, where she is responsible for the management and configuration of their emergency vehicle mobilising systems.

Jacqueline has been married to Hugh for almost forty glorious years and is a proud mother and doting grandmother. She lives by Psalms 107:1: "O give thanks unto the Lord, for He is good: for His mercy endureth for ever." In her free time, she loves to read, listen to music, socialise, travel and enjoy good food.

DEZRENE JONES-BEEZER

Dezrene Jones-Beezer was born in Mandeville, Manchester, Jamaica. Now based in the UK, she is married to Wayne Beezer and has two beautiful children, Rachael and Daniel Beezer. She is an Evangelist in her local church Bethel New Life, Coventry, UK, and is passionate about building people up spiritually and motivating them to maximise their growth in their relationships with Jesus.

Dezrene acquired a diploma with a B.S. in nursing with commendation and first-class honours from Birmingham City University. In August 2021, she enrolled in a three-year Bible study programme, hoping to gain more knowledge and be more rooted in and grounded by the Biblical truth and the word of God. She is a nurse and ward manager by trade and will be celebrating her 20th year in the profession in September 2023.

Dezrene recognises that a carer is a person who cares for others but sometimes never gets cared for and endeavours to raise awareness of the importance of 'caring for the carer', emphasising that the needs of carers must garner more attention and support. She is currently working on relaunching John's Campaign, which supports extended visiting rights for family carers in hospitals to ensure continuous care and alleviation of anxiety, with the goal of introducing it to other hospitals and care homes over time.

Dezrene enjoys travelling, spending time with family, listening to music, cooking delicious family meals and relaxing the comfort of her own home. Dezrene adheres to her favourite saying, with an apt tweak to Henry Longfellow's original words, as she strives on: "The heights by great women reached and kept were not attained by sudden flight." It reminds her to hold on to her belief in hard work, which makes success attainable for anyone.

DR CAROL S. IGHOFOSE

Dr Carol S. Ighofose (née Douglas) is a mother, an evangelist, a general practitioner (GP), a company director, an author and a public speaker. To date, her authorship has focused on non-fiction health-related books tailored to a church and faith-based audience. As lead author in this work, she solidifies her authority in cardiovascular health, advocating passionately for wellbeing within her community. Recognised and honoured as a British Heart Foundation (BHF) Heart Hero Finalist in 2021, Dr Carol is deeply committed to empowering others.

With a remarkable career spanning over three decades, Dr Carol has extensive experience in various primary and secondary care settings. Currently serving as a sessional GP in Urgent/Primary Care in the UK, she has worked in diverse clinical specialties, including psychiatry, paediatrics, obstetrics and gynaecology; and has also been involved in medical research focusing on asthma, diabetes and cardiovascular disease.

Dr Carol's dedication to general wellbeing and women's empowerment is evident in her first two books. Following a personal journey through a heart attack over five years ago, she penned her first published work *Fearfully and Wonderfully Made: The Heart of the Matter!* (2018). This poignant work addresses gender health inequalities, specifically related to women and heart health. Her second book *Can Women Have It All?* (2022) delves into her own encounters with life's crises as a woman and reevaluates the age-old debate about women's roles in society and the expectations imposed upon them.

Throughout her life and career, Dr Carol's enduring testimony remains rooted in her unwavering faith in God. Her life's motto is Philippians 4:13: "I can do all things through Christ who strengthens me." Guided by this principle propelling her forward, she continues to make a profound impact on the lives of countless individuals, as a beacon of hope, empowerment and transformation.

Contact:
Carol@LydiMed.co.uk
www.drcarol.co.uk
https://www.linkedin.com/in/dr-carol-s-ighofose
https://www.facebook.com/carol.ighofose.5

ELAINE RICHARDS

Elaine was born and raised in Wolverhampton, England. Her parents, Easton and the late Maudeline Laird, were the inspirations for her work ethic.

As she grew up with three brothers, many assumed she would be the princess of the family, but she was certainly 'one of the boys'. She climbed trees, played football, changed a fuse and tinkered under the bonnet of a car, making her mother despair at times!

After attending high school, Elaine trained to become a RGN (registered general nurse), after which she undertook further training as a midwife, health visitor, contraception & sexual health nurse. She currently works as a general practice nurse in an inner city GP practice, where she uses all of her prior training to help her patients manage and improve their health.

Elaine loves to travel, and having worked in Riyadh, Saudi Arabia, as a midwife, she has never had her passion for travel unsatiated.

Growing up, Elaine attended Bethel All Saints Church, Wolverhampton, pastored by the late Overseer H U Powell, and for the last three decades has attended Bethel Manchester under the current leadership of Bishop David Miller. She has held several local, district and national roles in the youth, women and Sunday school departments of the church, and throughout her years has engaged in various public health presentations locally and nationally as well as internationally on zoom meetings.

Elaine has been married to her husband Neil since 1992. They have been blessed with two wonderful children - Isabel and Adrian, each of whom have become independent young adults and follow the Lord in their lives.

Elaine has come this far by faith, leaning on the Lord. To God be the glory!

SANDRA SIMMONDS-GOCAN

Sandra Simmonds-Gocan qualified in 1988 as a registered general nurse (RGN) upon completion of her studies at the Mid Surrey School of Nursing in Epsom, Surrey. Following her training, she returned to her birth city of Birmingham and worked in various hospital departments including A&E and medical and surgical wards. Sandra then worked in an infectious diseases and renal ward in Ipswich, Suffolk, and went on to work as a theatre anaesthetic and recovery nurse, after which she travelled to Canada and passed the Canadian nursing examination to qualify as a registered nurse (RN) in Canada. Here she had the privilege of undertaking care for the veterans of the Second World War and for Parkinson's and Huntington's patients.

Upon returning to the UK, Sandra worked in colorectal and genitourinary wards before earning a diploma in occupational health from the University of Warwick and taking a job in Birmingham as an occupational health advisor. Sandra completed her training in the Specialist Community Practitioner in School Nursing program (SCPHN) and earned a BSc (Hons) from the University of Wolverhampton; and received a diploma in asthma from Education for Health in Warwick. She subsequently qualified and worked for four years as a school nurse before she returned to occupational health and later started working in COVID-19 vaccine administration. She recently earned a graduate certificate in general practice nursing from Birmingham City University and is currently a qualified practice nurse working in a local GP surgery.

Sandra is an anointed worship leader and preacher of the Word of God. Sandra attended the Bethel Institute of Biblical Studies, served as the National Youth President in Bethel United Church of Jesus Christ UK from 1990 to 1991, and worked closely with the Presiding Bishop S A Dunn, Bishop G Edmund and Bishop M H Simmonds. Sandra has served as an usher in Bethel Telford for more than fifteen years and has recently been recommended by her pastor to be an Evangelist in the Lord's church. She has successfully organised the launch of coffee mornings at her local church with the help of other members. She was a member of the Bethel Mass Choir and also worked with the youth choir of Bethel Telford in the past. Sandra taught in the Bethel United School for Youth (BUSY) and also taught Sunday school at her local church. Outside her professional career, Sandra enjoys reading autobiographies and travelling with her family.

Sandra would like to thank her pastor Elder Raymond Narme and his family; her dearest husband Paul Gocan; her sons Joshua and Daniel and daughters Rianna and Jennisha; her grandchildren Mya, Monroe and Amias; her beloved late father Pastor Roy A Bell (1922-2008); her dearly beloved mum, Mother M Bell; her siblings, nieces and nephews; her local church family Bethel Telford; and lastly the national church family and her wonderful work colleagues (past and current) for their support and prayers throughout the process of turning this project into reality.

ELENE MAYNARD-SCANTLEBURY

Elene is a mother, wife and grandmother. She is also a member of the Beacon Evangelical Church where she runs a Dementia Café for people with dementia. She is a motivated and experienced member of Dementia UK where she has acquired extensive knowledge for people living with all different kinds of dementia. Her strong listening and communication skills have enabled her to cater to individual needs and prepare and deliver appropriate advice and information to dementia carers.

She is passionate about connecting the Afro-Caribbean community and has organised information events as well as given talks to and supported organisations which fundraise for Dementia UK. Her background in nursing and education has given her a wide range of experience in providing others, especially young people, with advice and information. Benefiting from this experience, she also founded the 2nd Generation Barbados Association in 1998 where the focus was on helping the Barbadian community with health and social care education. In her spare time she loves listening to music and planning and hosting events for both the local community and church.

DANIEL SIMMONDS

During his early years, Daniel's first church assembly was at Bethel Ipswich under the tutelage of Bishop Martin Howard Simmonds. Daniel then moved to Birmingham and attended Bethel Wellington under the teaching and preaching of Pastor Roy Alphonso Bell and Pastor Raymond Narme respectively. It was during this time that Daniel undertook his primary, secondary and post-secondary education. Daniel, who at one point was not interested in pursuing higher education, was compelled in his late-teens to study law at Birmingham City University.

After delving into various fields of law, Daniel formally began his legal career in banking and restructuring at Pinsent Masons LLP and moved on to work in various legal positions at Bevan Brittan, Eversheds Sutherland, Werdna Freight Services, Coventry University and currently High Speed Rail Two (HS2). Daniel's specialty is commercial law, and he delights in making use of his expertise for a diverse clientele.

Daniel has been a devoted musician in Bethel United Church of Jesus Christ (Apostolic) as well as serving as a minister in the Lord's church. Since his mid-teens, Daniel has had the high privilege of being invited to preach and teach the gospel of Jesus Christ nationally and internationally. Daniel is currently an active member of Bethel Hall Green under the leadership of Pastor (D) Leon Hepburn.

Daniel recognises that he would not be where or who he is today without his loving wife, Rianna; his beloved parents, Andrew and Sandra; his favourite brother, Joshua; his grandparents on both sides, Bishop and Mother Simmonds and Pastor Roy and Mother Bell; and all of his aunties, uncles and cousins.

Daniel's greatest achievement after coming to know Jesus Christ is, in his own words, being a husband to his beautiful wife Rianna of nearly three years now and a father to their wonderful son, Monroe.

DEAR VALUED READER,

Firstly, we extend our heartfelt gratitude for choosing our book. We genuinely hope that you enjoyed reading it, and that the content provided proves both insightful and beneficial for you.

Your support holds immense significance as we strive to fulfil our mission of raising awareness about dementia, particularly within the context of our church community. We kindly request that you consider sharing your thoughts by leaving an honest review on Amazon. This will greatly help us to reach a broader audience, enhance our visibility and also serves as inspiration for others navigating the complexities of this challenging subject.

To facilitate this, we have provided a convenient QR code and a direct link. Simply scan the code or visit the link to be directed to the review page on Amazon.

Your feedback is truly invaluable and plays a crucial role in our ongoing mission to make a positive impact and contribute to the collective efforts in addressing the profound challenges posed by dementia.

Thank you once again for your support and for being an integral part of our journey. God bless you.

Warm regards,
Carol, Joy, Sandra, Dezrene, Daniel, Elaine, Jacqueline and Elene

NOTES

NOTES

NOTES

Printed in Great Britain
by Amazon